To BRIAN

# Paul Tergat

*Running to the Limit*

Best Wishes

Tergat

D0973185

Jürg Wirz

# Paul Tergat

*Running to the Limit*

## His Life and His Training Secrets

*With Many Tips for Runners*

MEYER
& MEYER
SPORT

British Library Cataloguing in Publication Data
A catalogue record for this book is available from the British Library

Jürg Wirz
Paul Tergat – Running to the Limit
Oxford: Meyer & Meyer Sport (UK) Ltd., 2005
ISBN 1-84126-165-3

© 2005 by Meyer & Meyer Sport (UK) Ltd.
Aachen, Adelaide, Auckland, Budapest, Graz, Johannesburg,
New York, Olten (CH), Oxford, Singapore, Toronto
Member of the World
Sports Publishers' Association (WSPA)
www.w-s-p-a.org
Printed and bound by: TZ Verlag, Germany
ISBN 1-84126-165-3
E-Mail: verlag@m-m-sports.com
www.m-m-sports.com

# CONTENTS

# INTRODUCTION

*"Nothing is impossible if you try"*

PAUL TERGAT

He has fulfilled the "Kenyan dream." Paul Tergat grew up in a humble family as one of 17 children in a poor district called Baringo in the western highlands of the country. There were days he had to eat the ashes from the firewood. But he was ready to fight – to fight for a better life. And he succeeded. With his talent, his will and his determination he managed to reach unthinkable heights.

Out of nowhere, he achieved more than any other long-distance runner before him: five-time World Cross country Champion, two-time World half-marathon Champion, World Record holder on the track at 10,000m and on the road in half-marathon and marathon. He has won four silver medals at the Olympic games and the World Championships at 10,000m. All this makes Paul Tergat one of history's greatest athletes.

In 1992, he had his breakthrough at national level, we first met at Ngong racecourse outside Nairobi. One month later we were together in Boston when he experienced his first disappointment: He was not able to go for his first world title because of an injury. I was with him when he won his fist gold medal at the World Cross country Championships 1995 in Durham and his first World Championship bronze medal on the track the same year in Gothenborg. Since then we have met again and again in Kenya and all over the world. Now that I am living in Kenya the friendship is even more intense, not only to Paul but also to his wife Monica, who has supported him all the way in an incredible manner.

*Running to the Limit* addresses Paul Tergat's journey from poverty into the world of fame. You will read about all his successes and disappointments, his thoughts about sports and life. But at the same time, *Running to the Limit* is a guide for amateurs as well as ambitious athletes. Along with Tergat's career, from the beginner to the World Record holder, you will find tips and training programs for everyday runners, as well as for aces. It is the first time Paul Tergat and his longtime coach, Dr. Gabriele Rosa, the most successful marathon coach in the world, give inside information and details about their training philosophy and programs.

I feel privileged to have known Paul for thirteen years, and I am proud he calls me a close friend, not only because of his great performances as a sportsman but also because of his achievements as a philanthropist. He helped to develop his home area, he helps poor children in Africa as an UN Ambassador for the World Food Program, he engages himself in the fight against landmines, he is on the way to establishing a foundation that is supposed to assist the poorest people in his home country. Even if he has made millions of dollars through his running, even if he moves with elegance, fitted in a designer suit, in the glittering world of celebrities, he has never forgotten his background. He remains simple, a true gentleman. And this is what makes Paul Tergat so special.

Eldoret/Kenya, Spring 2005

Jürg Wirz

*Author Jürg Wirz and Paul Tergat at the World Championships 1995 in Gothenborg*

# Chapter 1

# THE DREAM DIDN'T COME TRUE

For the past three months or so, before the Olympics 2004, there was not even one day Paul Tergat was not thinking about the marathon in Athens. He wanted to win this race more than anything else. He did everything he could to get the Olympic gold, the only medal still missing in his great career as a long distance runner. He punished his body to the limit by covering up to 300 kilometers a week. It was the hardest training regimen ever, more than most other human beings can take.

*Only one medal is missing: the Olympic gold*

Two weeks before D-day in Athens, he went for his last test. The temperature gauge in Tergat's Toyota Land Cruiser settled at 29 degrees Centigrade and the sun was burning like fire in this part of the Great Rift Valley at Oletapesi, 70km south of Ngong Hills and 100km outside Nairobi. Tergat and his 12 training mates arrived at 11 a.m. in two vehicles for the final countdown: the last extremely demanding run before the Athens Olympics. The tarmac was equally hot at an altitude of 1200m above sea level. For Paul Tergat, the run ended one hour and 15 minutes later at Olepolos trading center, 21 kilometers away, and he looked as if he had come directly from the shower. Some of his fellow runners broke down and headed to the escort van while others stopped more than twice along the route exhausted to their bones.

Some sections of the road were so steep that the 4x4 vehicles struggled in second gear, reaching the top at an altitude of 1700m above sea level as recorded in the altimeter of the Toyota with a boiling engine. Tergat had to run the final 5km alone after Joshua Chelang'a dropped back. Chelang'a, Tergat's longtime friend and training partner, finished the Berlin Marathon one and a half months later in third position, running 2:07,05. But that day between Oletapesi and Olepolos after this brutal run, he was completely done and stammered: "Hiyo imeishe" – "it is over." Later, after drinking immense quantities of water and sodas, they joked a lot, happy to have concluded another punishing midday run under conditions worse than what the master would face in Athens. Paul Tergat was in the shape of his life.

But a few days before he traveled with his wife Monica to Athens, Tergat almost became the victim of an attack. Thieves were waiting for him at the gate of his Ngong home. It was the day he was supposed to pick up his running colleague, Joshua Chelang'a, from the airport, but Tergat decided to send only his driver and another man, and it seems this was his luck. The thieves robbed Chelang'a of his prize money from Europe and all his belongings and forced the driver and the other man to a nearby forest where the two were left. The thieves disappeared with the Land Cruiser worth between $ 30,000 and $ 40,000 US. Who knows what would have happened to Tergat if he had been in the car?

It was a real shock for Tergat, but when he was in Athens, he did not think about this incident anymore. Now all his focus was on the marathon. And when he lined up with all the other favorites on August 29, the last day of the 2004 Olympics, at 6 p.m., he was physically and mentally ready for the 42.195 kilometers to come. But it wasn't to be; When the leading group entered the last quarter of the race, the Kenyan was not able to follow the pace anymore and dropped back. After 42.195 kilometers, he entered Panathinaikon Stadium in a disappointing tenth position.

**P.T.:** *"The most important thing for me is that I was able to finish the race, the Olympic marathon in Athens was a very important moment in my life. It was maybe the most important race in my career, at least the last major one, my last chance to win the Olympic gold. I worked so, so hard to achieve this last target, I didn't leave anything to chance. I was absolutely ready. And as the race progressed, I felt more and more confident. Everything went according to plan. But when we reached the water station at kilometer 30, I missed my bottle. I knew I could not wait for another five kilometers where I had again my own drink, by the way, water with glucose, I knew in this heat and humidity it would have been deadly. So I had to take the water which the organizers supplied. Unfortunately this water was very cold. It did not take even two minutes when my stomach started cramping. First it was a cramp and than a stitch. It was very painful. Nevertheless I didn't panic and thought it might disappear. But it didn't. I reduced the pace – it persisted. I tried to breathe deeply and to massage the pain away. Nothing helped. I could not follow the pace of the leading group anymore. When I realized the race was gone, my dream was destroyed, I was very upset, I was angry. I sacrificed so much for my last Olympic opportunity. It was so hard to accept what happened. I mean if you are not well prepared, if other competitors are stronger than you, you have to accept it. If you ran your heart out and still you cannot make it, if you gave your best and you lose, that's okay. But it was in fact such a stupid accident that robbed me of my fair chance.*

*I didn't want to think of dropping out. I wanted to finish. Never in my whole career have I dropped out from a race. I never entered a race when I was not in a good form. If I know I cannot give my best, I prefer staying at home. That is me. I know many athletes, they go to a race even if they are not in shape. Me, I could never do this. I am a professional athlete. If an organizer decides to spend money on me, I have the responsibility to give him the best possible equivalent. Even if I was really disturbed mentally, I knew I am going to finish. I didn't want to throw in the towel. Not even for one second I thought I might quit. I was not afraid to lose. In championships there are always winners and losers. When you are into the sports this is something you have to accept. I felt my responsibility for my country but also for myself as Paul Tergat. The only thing that really bothered me was that I was not able to run my race and to show my real potential.*

*I am a strong believer that a man is not only measured by his performances but also by his achievements. Finishing the race was a big achievement for me. Even if I was only number 10, I was proud of myself, for me personally it was a victory. It will give me the necessary strength to go on with my mission. I will continue my career for at least two or three more big city marathons. The passion is still the same as that time when I began my running career."*

Paul Tergat still wants to win some major marathons. He thinks it is not enough to have won only the Berlin marathon where he broke the World Record. He wants to win and run another fast time. But he knows it will not be easy because he needs to have somebody who is pushing him at least to 37 or 38km. That means somebody who is able to run 2 hours 7 minutes himself. And these athletes usually prefer to go for the victory rather than being rabbits. Tergat is convinced that nobody can break the World Record when he is already alone after 30 or 35 kilometers.

When will he retire? As of spring 2005, he doesn't know himself and he doesn't want to fix a date. But he is aware that now that he is almost 36, the body may start rejecting this immense torture. He had already a first warning signal when he suffered a calf muscle injury while preparing for London in 2004 and finally had to quit the race. It was his first injury after twelve years!

Irrespective of his Olympic failure in Athens and of what he will still achieve as a runner, Paul Tergat will be remembered as one of the greatest long distance runners of all time.

## TERGAT'S THOUGHTS

- Never go to a race when the training was not really good, when you have a health problem or an injury, even a small one.

- When you decide to participate in a race, you have to be ready to give your best.

- Plan your races some months in advance. Preparing for a race means not only the physical training, it means also the right mental preparation. When we talk about marathon, we talk about a discipline that is a punishment for your body. If you are not prepared mentally, you will not succeed.

- Even when you feel you cannot achieve your goal, never drop out of a race. When you drop out once you will do it again. The only reason for not finishing a race is a health problem, e.g. dehydration, or an injury.

# HOW EVERYTHING BEGAN

Even without winning the Olympic marathon in Athens, Paul Tergat remains an outstanding athlete, the most complete runner of modern times. He is a five-time World Champion in cross country and has won two times in the half-marathon. He won four silver medals at major championships, two at the world's and two at the Olympics, all in the 10,000m. He broke World Records on the track (10,000m, 1997) and on the road (15 km, 1994; half-marathon, 1998; marathon, 2003). All this helped him to be one of the richest athletes in the world. What an achievement for somebody who grew up in a small town called Riwo in Baringo District where no other international runner came from before him. The people from Baringo are Tugen, a tribe who, like the Keyio, the Marakwet, the Nandi and the Kipsigis, belong to the Kalenjin.

When he first entered the limelight in 1992, there were a number of other Kenyan athletes, all younger than him, among them Matthew Birir, Olympic Champion in the 3,000m steeplechase, Moses Kiptanui, three-time World Champion in the 3,000m steeplechase and Ismael Kirui, two-time World Champion in the 5,000m: They are all retired, but Tergat is still going strong.

**P.T.:** *"I come from an extended family. We were 17, together with the half brothers and sisters. My father had three wives, something what was very common at that time in the rural population. Our houses were simple huts with thatch. We were really poor. Sometimes when I came home from school there was no food. That's why I preferred staying with some friends. Honestly, life was very tough. I believe very much that this very humble background made me what I am and gave me the strength for being at the top of my sport for so many years."*

*Tergat with his grandmother, who was over 90 years old when the picture was taken*

Paul attended Riwo Primary School for eight years. He was a very bright pupil. He calls it a gift God gave him. Running to school "the Kenyan way?" Not at all! The school was only 2 kilometers from his home. When he was 16, he joined Kapkakwa Boys High School. Most of the time there was a school bus that picked him at home.

**P.T.:** *"My parents didn't have the money for paying my school fees. I didn't want to stay at home. I knew education is the key for everything. So I had to strike a deal with the headmaster. I asked him to waive the fees and I assured him I was going to refund everything as soon as I earned my first money. The teacher liked me very much and he agreed. In fact, when I joined the army I went back to the school and refunded all the fees that had accumulated in the course of the years."*

As far as he knew then he didn't have a talent for running. In primary school, they were just running a little bit around the playing field. They already had some kind of competitions but little Tergat always preferred running in the relay together with others, not against them. It never occurred to him that he was more gifted than his classmates. He also liked playing soccer and volleyball. It was in high school when he started running. He participated in a number of school competitions and was doing quite well, still without any training.

**P.T.:** *"I had a lot of passion for running. Always when I got a newspaper and there was a story about athletics I used to cut it out. I loved running but there was no role model in my home area I could emulate. My dream was to become a soldier or let's say a career in the military. But I remember very well one day in 1987 when I was 18 my dad took me and my elder brother, John, to Nairobi where we were watching the 4th African Championships. I loved it. It made a great impression on me. From that day on I wanted to be a runner myself."*

In 1990, Paul Tergat joined the military and that is where he became a runner.

# TERGAT'S TIPS FOR BEGINNERS

First you have to ask yourself what your personal goal in running is. If you want to be a champion, you can skip this chapter. Here we talk to the beginners, people who are not fit but intend to change their lifestyle and improve their health. To come to the point: Fun and fitness should always be the principle goals. Sometimes you may have to work quite hard to achieve your goals, but the pleasure you get from achieving them will make up for the pain. The author of this book was quite a good runner on a national level as a junior but had to give it up because of a serious back problem. This is when he started smoking cigarettes, first one pack a day, then two and at the end of a "ten-year smoking career" he consumed up to three packs a day – especially on the days when he had night shift as an editor.

He was 30 when he stopped smoking and instead started to go for jogging: first only a few hundred meters, then a few kilometers, and after four years, he ran his first marathon.

The author's first marathon was in 1984 in New York, the year when even the Italian winner Orlando Pizzolato had to stop several times because of the extreme weather conditions and finally crossed the line in 2:14:53, the slowest time in the history of the NYCM. Despite this tough debut, the author has since run many marathons all over the world. It is enjoyable to be a runner, to be able to run for one or two hours through the open country without getting tired. What an accomplishment to be strong and fit.

And now, you too, have decided to do something for your fitness. Maybe the early morning sprint to the bus station showed you how poor your physical condition is. Or going upstairs in a house where there was no elevator. There are everyday experiences that are opening our eyes and giving us a kind of a wake-up call. In this chapter, we will show you how you can run 30 minutes uninterrupted within 12 weeks – even if you are far from being a talent in running.

The good thing with running is you can do it everywhere and at every time.

*A landscape made for running*

You don't need expensive equipment like in many other sports. If you want to become a runner, you need only two things: good running shoes and an outfit adequate to the specific weather conditions. What is meant by "good shoes?" To come to the point: The most expensive aren't necessarily the best. Consult a specialist shop where they are able to check your feet on a podoscope. They should even have you to run on a treadmill or in front of the shop. That's how an experienced seller can identify your running style. Let them show you all the models that are possible for you. Remember: Women do need different shoes! Try the shoes on with special running socks and don't buy shoes too small. When you stand, there should be at least one centimeter of space in front of the toes.

The fabrics used in modern sports clothes are very functional. There is no bad weather for running, there is only the wrong outfit. Cotton t-shirts, saturated with sweat or rain water, are definitely out. The fabrics used for running transport the sweat away from your body and protect you from catching a cold at the same time. Provided you don't start with your running program in the deepest winter, you will need only the following items:

## Your first running outfit

- running shoes
- running socks
- shorts and/or tights
- singlet or functional t-shirt
- rain jacket

One thing we would like to remind you before you rush out of your house full of enthusiasm and thirst for action is that running is not as simple as one may think. For the first 10 or 20 training sessions you might not feel like a highly gifted runner but more like a heavy sack of cement. Don't get discouraged! Other beginners feel exactly the same. Look for like-minded people or join a jogging group, then the start will be much easier. Together everything is easier! By the way, even the Kenyan top runners prefer training in a group, because it is less demanding and tiring.

It is for your own good to follow a program for beginners that is tried and tested. Following the method below, you will be able to run, after 12 weeks, 30 minutes or approximately 5 kilometers non-stop and that's not bad at all!

# RUNNING 30 MINUTES IN 12 WEEKS

Note for the training programs: ' = minutes, " = seconds

## WEEK 1

Tue:    10' speed walking and stretching;
        3x 1' easy jogging, 2' speed walking in-
        between; stretching

Thu:    same as Tuesday

Sun:    10' speed walking and stretching;
        3x 2' easy jogging, 2' walking in-between;
        stretching

## WEEK 2

Tue:    10' speed walking and stretching; 3x 2'
        jogging, 1' walking in-between; stretching

Thu:    10' speed walking and stretching; 1-2-3-2-1'
        jogging, 1' walking in-between; stretching

Sun:    10' speed walking and stretching; one lap on
        a fitness trail (with strength exercises),
        jogging from one exercise point to the other;
        alternatives: aqua gym (gym exercises in the
        water and deep water running) or strength
        program (easy jogging between the exercises);
        stretching

# WEEK 3

| | |
|---|---|
| Tue: | 10' speed walking and stretching; 3x 3' jogging, 1-2' walking in-between; stretching |
| Thu: | 10' walking and stretching; 3x 3' jogging, 1-2' walking in-between; stretching |
| Sun: | same as Thursday |

# WEEK 4

| | |
|---|---|
| Tue: | 10' speed walking and stretching; 2-3-4-5-4-3-2' jogging, 1-2' walking in-between; stretching |
| Thu: | 10' speed walking and stretching; 5-8-5' jogging, 1-2' walking in-between; stretching |
| Sun: | 10-15' easy jogging or walking and stretching; one lap on a fitness trail (all the exercises; jogging from one exercise point to the other); alternatives: aqua gym or strength program; stretching |

# WEEK 5

| Tue: | 10' speed walking and stretching; 6-10x 3' jogging, 1' speed walking in-between; stretching |
|------|---|
| Thu: | 10' easy jogging or walking and stretching; 3x 10' jogging, 2' speed walking in-between; stretching |
| Sun: | 10-15' easy jogging or walking and stretching; during 30' change between 2' running and 1' easy jogging; stretching |

# WEEK 6

| Tue: | 10-15' easy jogging or walking and stretching; 3x 10' running, 2' easy jogging in-between; stretching |
|------|---|
| Thu: | 10-15' easy jogging or walking and stretching; 2x 15' running, 3-5' walking in-between; stretching |
| Sun: | 10-15' easy jogging or walking and stretching; 3x 10' running, 1'speed walking in-between; stretching |

# WEEK 7

Tue:      10-15' easy jogging or walking and stretching;
2x 15-20' running, 5' break in-between with
stretching; stretching

Thu:      10-15' easy jogging or walking and stretching;
20' running, the last 5' easy; stretching

Sun:      same as Thursday

# WEEK 8

Tue:      10-15' easy jogging or walking and stretching;
3x 10' easy jogging, 2' speed walking
in-between; stretching

Thu:      10-15' easy jogging or walking and stretching;
20-30' running on a hilly course (walking
where it is too steep); stretching

Sun:      10-15' easy jogging or walking and stretching;
30' running, last 5' easy; stretching

# WEEK 9

| | |
|---|---|
| Tue: | 10-15' easy jogging or walking and stretching; 2x 15' running, 2' speed walking in-between; stretching |
| Thu: | 10-15' easy jogging or walking and stretching; 6-10x 1' running, 1' very easy jogging or speed walking in-between; 5-10' easy jogging; stretching |
| Sun: | 10-15' easy jogging or walking and stretching; 30-40' easy running; stretching |

# WEEK 10

| | |
|---|---|
| Tue: | 10-15' easy jogging or walking and stretching; 2x 20' running, 2' speed walking in-between; stretching |
| Thu: | 10-15' easy jogging or walking and stretching; 30-40' easy running; stretching |
| Sun: | same as Tuesday |

# WEEK 11

Tue: 10-15' easy jogging or walking and stretching; change between 2-3' running and 2-3' speed walking (approx. 30'); 5-10' easy jogging or walking; stretching

Thu: 10-15' easy jogging or walking and stretching; 2x 15' easy jogging, 2' speed walking in-between; stretching

Sun: 10-15' easy jogging or walking and stretching; 30-40' running on a hilly course (walking where it is too steep); stretching, last 5' easy; stretching

# WEEK 12

Tue: 10-15' easy jogging or walking and stretching; 3x 10' running, 2 min speed walking in-between; stretching

Thu: 10-15' easy jogging or walking and stretching; 20-30' very easy jogging; stretching

Sun: 10' easy jogging or walking and stretching; 30' running; stretching

Important: A strength program (e.g., exercises with your own body, gym or aqua gym) should be included 1-2 times a week in the training program.

## STATIC AND DYNAMIC STRETCHING

**Static stretching:** Hold the position for 30-60 sec. You feel a tension in the stretched muscle but no pain. Static stretching can be done everywhere: after the training, at home, in the office, in the bus or on the train. After the training, static stretching normalizes the muscle tension. That's why static stretching is recommended for relaxing but not immediately before fast training or competition.

**Dynamic stretching:** Recommended before fast training or competition. Bring the muscle in a position in which you feel a slight tension. In this position, 5-10 short, swinging movements have to be done. For the warm-up, the traditional gymnastic exercises are also suitable.

*Paul Tergat on the way to his first national title in February 1992. Also on the picture: the late Richard Chelimo (left) and William Koech (middle)*

*First prize money at the IAAF Cross country in Nairobi*

# Chapter 3

# WITHIN ONE YEAR AT THE TOP

Paul Tergat didn't know he would become a great athlete until he joined the military in 1990. First, he had to go for basic military training for nine months in Eldoret.

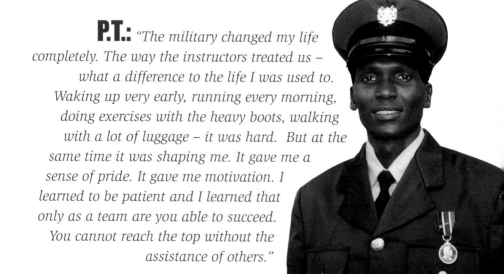

**P.T.:** *"The military changed my life completely. The way the instructors treated us – what a difference to the life I was used to. Waking up very early, running every morning, doing exercises with the heavy boots, walking with a lot of luggage – it was hard. But at the same time it was shaping me. It gave me a sense of pride. It gave me motivation. I learned to be patient and I learned that only as a team are you able to succeed. You cannot reach the top without the assistance of others."*

In December 1990 he was transferred to Nairobi where he joined the Air Force. One full year was spent on special training with a lot of classes. His special subject was supplying, and he was at the central supply depot (CSD), where they were distributing not only spare parts and equipment but also stationeries for the whole Air Force. He was very proud to be part of the Air Force where, at that time, even Moses Tanui, 1991 World Champion at 10,000m and later one of the best marathoners in the world, and William Tanui, 1992 Olympic Champion at 800m, were serving. The army was, besides prisons and police, the only institution where a talented Kenyan athlete could improve his running. Most of the strong athletes came from the military. There were no camps, sponsored by shoe companies or foreigners. Ten years later all the important European agents have established their own camps – there were more than 30 in early 2005. And some of the agents organize their own races where they recruit the talents.

*Jogging to the start of the "Nationals": in white the athletes of the Armed Forces*

Now Paul Tergat became a real runner. In Nairobi, he ran every morning in a big group, always the same 15 kilometers around the Air Force Base and sometimes again in the evening. It was more or less always the same pace, nothing but endurance training. He still had to attend some lessons and didn't want to exhaust himself. And frankly he had no idea about training at that time. But then came the first inter-unit race. Tergat was far behind but the coach was impressed the way this newcomer was running and invited him to the training camp where the "top guns" were preparing for three months for the Armed Forces Championships. For the first time, he could be near his heroes. They trained together, they slept in the same tents, shared the same meals and were not in any way different from him. They were also human. It is then he found he could keep up with them.

**P.T.:** *"When they gave me the opportunity to train with the best, I took it as my big chance. I started to work really hard. In these few months at the end of 1991 and beginning of 1992, I followed for the first time a proper training program with long runs, fartlek, hill-work, etc., three times a day, six days a week. And when we finished the official training, I sometimes ran some more kilometers on my own."*

The Armed Forces Cross country Championships were held at Nanyuki. Even if he had been still very far behind in training and in some local races, Tergat managed to finish third.

Two months later he was on the top of the Kenyan running scene. He won the National Cross country Championships at Ngong racecourse by a big margin and after another week he also won the IAAF Cross, held at the same venue.

It was the first time he received some money: 60,000 Ksh, that time approximately $ 1,000 US, for the 22-year-old Tergat – a very big amount.

*With his first money Tergat built this house for his mother at Riwo*

By now Tergat had overtaken his heroes through sheer hard work and determination. He became the big favorite for the World Cross country Championships in Boston. Then came an unfortunate injury. They ran on the tarmac, something that Tergat had never done before, because there was snow everywhere. All of a sudden, he felt a twitch in his calf muscle. First it was just a slight pain but in the evening he could not even walk. Suddenly, he knew he would be out for the race.

**P.T.:** *"I was stressed. It was a terrible experience. I couldn't believe what happened to me. I thought this was the end of everything. To be there without being able to run made me cry. I will never forget it in my life. But the worst was still to come. When we were back in Kenya nobody from the Federation cared about me. Nobody helped me to get the right treatment. And it was the Swiss journalist Jürg Wirz who was the first who offered his help. I realized then that in this world you have a few friends you must treasure at all times."*

Doctor Gabriele Rosa who had just started to coach some Kenyan athletes, remembered this young talent he saw running and winning in Nairobi, too. He invited Tergat to his clinic in the Italian town of Brescia for the treatment. That was the beginning of a very successful collaboration. But it took Paul Tergat two years to recover completely from the injury and the mental pain he had suffered.

# TERGAT'S TIPS FOR THE FIRST COMPETITION

Some time ago you started to run. Within a few months you gained control of the 5km. Now you might think about testing your fitness in a road race. What about a competition at 10 or even 15 kilometers? You think you will be ready? One thing before we go into the details: Don't try a distance that you are not used to from training.

# HOW TO MAKE YOUR FIRST RACE A SUCCESS

- For your first race, you should choose an easy course with as few uphill sections as possible.

- Take your last meal – easily digestible – 3 or 4 hours before the start of your race. Drink enough! In the last 1 or 2 hours you can still go for an energy bar and water or a sports drink.

- Don't run in new shoes. Use the ones you have used already in training.

- Don't warm up for a long time. Ten minutes of easy jogging and a few dynamic stretching exercises are enough.

- Line up in the last third of the field. Do this so you don't stand in the way of faster runners and so it will be easier for you to find your race pace on the first kilometer.

- Try to run in a comfortable pace from the beginning. Don't follow others. Most of the runners, even much more experienced ones than you are, begin too fast.

- If you are able to, overtake some runners on the last kilometer. It will help you to make your first race a real success.

Now that you are a real runner, the time has come for you to give a few thoughts about your running style. With a good running technique you can save energy and avoid injuries.

Every person develops a very unique and individual running style. Posture and running styles reflect your physique and the feeling you have for your body. We run the way we feel. The bigger your ambitions are, the more important are some regularities and basic principles. A good running technique makes you run faster. Economical running means running with less effort and less energy loss. The exercises for improving the running technique (so-called "running school", see the following pages) are very effective and should be included in your training at least once a week. To do this, look for a track with little gradient. After a 10-minute warm-up you should begin with the individual exercises (20 sec for each). Jog back after the first exercise and do the second, etc. After finishing the "running school" (10-20 min), you can go for your run.

## Ankle joint

Easy jogging with very short steps and high frequency. Lift the toes as little as possible from the ground, the movements are supposed to come from the ankle joints. Stretch the trailing leg.

## Skipping

Easy jogging. Lift the left and the right knee alternatively up to a horizontal line. The upper part of the body remains upright.

## Heels up

Easy jogging. With the left and the right heel you touch alternatively your buttocks. The thigh remains in a vertical position, the upper part of the body should remain upright.

## Jumping strides

Lengthen your strides by pushing strongly from the ground. The stride is supposed to get longer and higher, knees up to the horizontal line.

## Accelerations

Accelerate the pace continuously over a distance of 80 to 100 meters. Accelerations are recommended at the end of a "running school" or after a run.

**Head:** The head is supposed to be in an upright position on the shoulders, relaxed, looking straight ahead.

**Shoulders:** Don't lift up the shoulders, they are supposed to be relaxed.

**Arms:** Forearm and upper arm should form a right angle that remains throughout the arm movement.

**Hands:** The hands are slightly open, the fingers are relaxed, the thumb lies on the forefinger

**Trunk:** The trunk has to stabilize the whole running movement. It is supposed to be bent slightly in front but upright.

**Hips/legs:** The strides are flowing but not too big. When you push from the ground, the knee and the hips have to be stretched.

**Foot:** The foot touches the ground a little bit in front of the body's axis. When you touch down, almost all the positions are possible: landing on the heel, the middle foot or the fore foot.

## ADAPT TO THE TERRAIN

When you are **running uphill,** shorten your strides and push the foot with more intensity from the ground. If you push with the ankle joints, the thigh muscles will get a welcome relief. The arms have to support the movements rigorously. Bend the upper part of the body a little bit more in front compared with running on the flat.

**Running downhill** brings the biggest strain for your body, especially the joints and the back. (Sore muscles are a result of running downhill and not from running uphill.) Reduce the pace when you are running downhill. When you are running downhill the foot has to touch the ground in a flat position on the outside. Lean slightly back with the upper part of the body.

# Chapter 4

# KING OF CROSS COUNTRY AND HALF-MARATHON

In September 1992, Paul Tergat was back in action and came in fifth at the inaugural World Half-marathon Championships in Newcastle. But when the next World Cross was held in Amorebieta in Spain he was still not in the shape of the previous year. The man of the moment was William Sigei, a 23-year-old Air Force corporal from Kericho. Sigei had won the Kenyan Armed Forces and the National Championships and became World Champion in Spain.

Tergat's time came 1995 at Durham (GBR). Sigei who had won also in 1994 was out injured, and head coach Mike Kosgei confirmed that Paul Tergat was the man to watch. The tall Kenyan had set a world road best at 15km in Budapest and won the 1995 Kenyan cross country title by a margin of 15 seconds. James "Rambo" Songok and Ismael Kirui were assigned as the main pacemakers.

*National coach Mike Kosgei in his simple room at the Embu training camp*

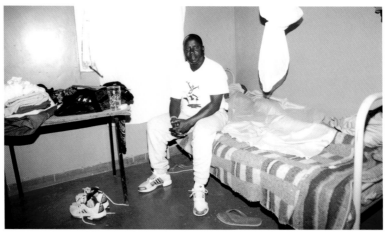

Tergat took over just before the bell and was not caught. Haile Gebrselassie who had won his only cross country medal on the senior level, a bronze, in the previous year at Budapest, finished fourth behind Kirui and the Moroccan Salah Hissou.

Now the ice was broken. Tergat became almost invincible. His self-confidence was growing more and more with every year and every win: 1996 at Stellenbosch (RSA) he was 12 seconds ahead of Hissou. 1997 in the Italian city of Turin, Hissou, that time the World Record holder at 10,000m, managed to stay with Tergat until the final 300m. "It was the hardest of my three victories," admitted Tergat after reaching the finish with a relatively scant margin of two seconds.

STELLENBOSCH 1996

URIN 1997

# MILANO 1998

# TRAINING, EATING AND SLEEPING

In Kenya, cross country plays a very important role because all the coaches believe this is the best preparation for the track season, for middle distance runners, as well as the long distance runners. Cross country is a kind of religion. No wonder Kenyans have dominated this sport so much. In the 31 years of the World Championships (1973-2004), Kenyans have won 204 medals, followed by Ethiopia (171) and the United States (57) and a record of 58 team titles. In 1991, 1993, 1995 and 1996, Kenya swept all the available team titles. The man who has won the most number of gold medals in the history of the World Championships is Paul Tergat with 13, including five individual and eight teams medals.

When the cross country national team prepares for the World Championships at Embu, on the slopes of Mount Kenya, the training regime is tough. The days are made up of training, eating and sleeping, six times a week. Sunday is a rest day. According to national coach Mike Kosgei, "this is when the athletes have to pray and ask God for more energy."

When there is an early morning run at 6 a.m., the athletes have breakfast at 7:30 and then relax or sleep for another two hours. After the 10 o'clock training (always the main training of the day), they drink tea.

Lunch is at 1 p.m., followed again by relaxing/sleeping before the training at 4 p.m. (Kosgei: "Rest is very important after eating"). Supper is at 7:30 p.m. After supper, there is also time for talking about the training of the day and next day's program. ("When somebody is lying in the bed, he can already think about the fartlek of tomorrow.") Sometimes there is still time for a little bit of TV – at least the national news. At 9 or 9:30 p.m. everybody is asleep.

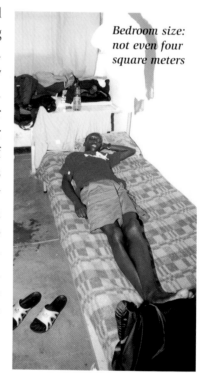

*Bedroom size: not even four square meters*

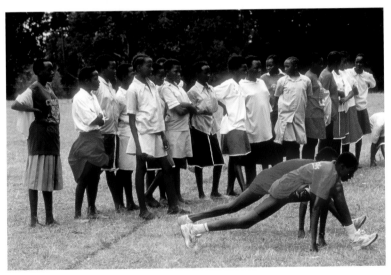

The main reason the Kenyans have their main training at 10 a.m. according to Kosgei is "this is the time of the day when you still have a lot of energy. The other point: If you wait until 4 in the afternoon for the hard session, you don't have enough time for recovery. You cannot train hard, eat and then go to bed."

This was the program Paul Tergat followed during the years he was winning the World Championships.

# WEEK 1

**Mon:** 6 a.m.: - / 10 a.m.: 25km easy run / 4 p.m.: -

**Tue:** 6 a.m.: - / 10 a.m.: 10km easy run + flexibility / 4 p.m.: 4km warm-up + 30' circuit training (strength)

**We:** 6 a.m.: 45' easy run / 10 a.m.: 15km medium pace + stretching / 4 p.m.: 10km easy run + flexibility

**Thu:** 6 a.m.: 45' easy run / 10 a.m.: 8km high speed (90-95% effort for tuning the muscles)/ 4 p.m.: 10km easy run + flexibility

**Fri:** 6 a.m.: - / 10 a.m.: 18km medium pace / 4 p.m.: 6km body coordination + jogging (to break the lactate acid)

**Sat:** 6 a.m.: 45' easy run / 10 a.m.: 10km fartlek (3-2-1-1/2' fast with 3/2/1/1' recovery) / 4 p.m.: 10km easy run

**Sun:** church / rest

# WEEK 2

**Mon:**  6 a.m.: - / 10 a.m.: 18km easy run / 4 p.m.: 10km medium pace

**Tue:**  6 a.m.: 45' easy run / 10 a.m.: 6km warm-up, 25 x 200m speed (flat), 4km jogging / 4 p.m.: 10km easy run

**Wed:**  6 a.m.: 45' easy run / 10 a.m.: 15km medium pace / 4 p.m.: 10km easy run

**Thu:**  6 a.m.: 45' easy run / 10 a.m.: 8km jogging, 25 x 200m steep hill (75-80% effort, jogging back), warm-down / 4 p.m.: 11km easy run

**Fri:**  6 a.m.: - / 10 a.m.: 20km easy run / 4 p.m.: -

**Sat:**  6 a.m.: 45' easy run / 10 a.m.: 15km easy fartlek (3-2-1-1/2' fast with 3-2-1/1' recovery), stretching

**Sun:**  church / rest

Mon:     6 a.m.: - / 10 a.m.: 30km regeneration (easy)/
4 p.m.: -

Tue:     6 a.m.: - / 10 a.m.: 15km medium pace /
4 p.m.: 10km easy run + gymnastic exercises

Wed:     6 a.m.: 45' easy run / 10 a.m.: 12km high
speed + flexibility / 4 p.m.: 8km easy
jogging + gymnastic

Thu:     6 a.m.: - / 10 a.m.: 20km regeneration /
4 p.m.: 6km jogging on the grass + stretching

Fri:     6 a.m.: 45' easy run / 10 a.m.: 8km warm-up,
25 x 100m hill (less steep, shorter,
75-80% effort, jogging back), warm-down /
4 p.m.: 15km easy run

Sat:     6 a.m.: - / 10 a.m.: 18km medium pace +
flexibility / 4 p.m.: 13km easy jogging

Sun:     church / rest

# WEEK 4 (week of travel and competition)

Mon:    6 a.m.: - / 10 a.m.: 10km easy run / 4 p.m.:
        8km warm-up + flexibility

Tue:    6 a.m.: 45' easy run / 10 a.m.: 10km medium
        pace / 4 p.m.: 6km easy jogging

Wed:    Day of traveling. After arrival: 12km running
        in the group (on the course)

Thu:    3 p.m.: 15km easy

Fri:    12 a.m.: jogging on the course

Sat:    WORLD CHAMPIONSHIPS

One year later at Marrakesh (MOR), Paul Tergat matched John Ngugi's formidable record of four consecutive wins without taking the lead until the finish line was in sight. He glided clear to win comfortably ahead of his teammate, Paul Koech. What a difference in the style when they hammered into the straight: The shorter Koech whose paddling arm action contrasted with Tergat's upright elegance. After 12,000 meters there were five seconds between the two. It was 1999 in Belfast when Tergat crowned himself with the fifth title in a row, a feat no other athlete had ever achieved.

*1999 in Belfast:*
*Warm-up*
*as a team*

This time his countryman Patrick Ivuti came second. Tergat would later describe the course as "the toughest yet." Not only did he win a fifth individual title, but he also collected a seventh successive team gold and guaranteed himself a place in the gallery of the immortals on this 25 March.

**P.T.:** *"I am a countryman. In cross country I felt at home. These are the kind of races I first did when I started running and where I celebrated my first victories. Cross country is what I always liked most. It was my world, my passion. When I was in shape, I knew nobody could beat me regardless of the weather and the surface. It didn't matter if it was muddy or dry, hilly or flat. I am very proud to be a five-time winner. Before the IAAF introduced the short course in 1998, all the world class athletes from 1500m to marathon were in the same race. The World Cross country Championship was the toughest distance race in the world to win."*

Tergat won five times in a row, and he could or would have added a sixth crown in 2000 at Vilamoura. But there he used too much energy in endless discussions the night before the race, having meetings with the team officials, debating the inclusion of Charles Kamathi on the team. Kamathi was the leader of the IAAF world cross challenge standings, but had finished only 13th in the Kenyan Championships. However, Kamathi had beaten Tergat three times during the winter. The Kenyan officials had declared Kamathi and left out Joshua Chelang'a, who was fourth one year earlier in Belfast and eighth in the "Nationals."

*Tergat and Joshua Chelang'a*

It transpired that the Kenyan officials had thought Kamathi could compete as a non-scorer, since he led the cross challenge. However, the IAAF had changed the rule about individual entries, so Kenya could start with only six men. Tergat, among others, wanted Chelang'a, who was also with Fila and would have been an important pacemaker, to be included on the team. But the Kenyan officials gave preference to Kamathi and decided in a way also against the "King of X." When it came to the race the Kenyans had no team tactics, nobody was ready to sacrifice his chances for the team leader, and there was no game plan at all. And so Tergat finished only third, two seconds behind the Morocco born Belgian Mohammed Mourhit and one behind the Ethiopian Assefa Mezegebu. Tergat is still convinced that the Kenyan team officials were stealing the sixth world title from him. And he still gets angry when he talks about the "night of Vilamoura."

**P.T.:** *"I have also some weak points. And my weakest point is that I am very emotional. If something is not going according to plan it disturbs me a lot and can even throw me out of gear. I was not able to concentrate on the race anymore. We discussed almost all night long with the team officials. And when one of them, somebody who has never been a runner in his life, told me my job would be only running, I was really upset. These people travel around the world but don't even know how important the teamwork is, especially when it comes to cross country. All my five titles I had won also because of the help of my teammates. It was in the morning at 9 o'clock, only two hours before the race, when we finally decided to run – only because of our country. After the world X, I asked for a meeting with chairman Isaiah Kiplagat but five years later I am still* *waiting for it. By the way: Chelang'a had not only been stronger than Kamathi at the Nationals in Nairobi but also in the training camp."*

At Vilamoura the Kenyans ran for the first time without a team tactic. Not only because of the discussions during the night before but also because of a new phenomenon. Personal agents had become more important than national pride. The more money entered the sport the more the athletes became selfish.

**P.T.:** *"When you have success, you are much envied. All of a sudden friends turn against you."*

*Five times at the top in Sao Paulo*

*Paul Tergat at the
"Nationals" in 2000*

After the nightmare of Vilamoura, Tergat stayed in Portugal for another week and participated at the half-marathon of Lisbon. There he ran his frustration out of his body with a new World Best. His time of 59:06 was 11 seconds faster than his own record from two years earlier. In 2000, statisticians around the world were still discussing if the time from Lisbon should be recognized as a world best and even five years later, the Association of Track & Field Statisticians, ATFS, uses two official records: 59:17 (Milan 1998) and 59:06 (Lisbon 2000, with the addendum 40m downhill). The IAAF recognizes only the 59:17.

In his career as a half-marathon runner, which brought him two World Championship titles in 1999 and 2000, Tergat had even broken the 59-minute barrier once: 58:51 in the Stramilano in 1996. But the time was not recognized when an official check of the course brought to light that it was short by 49 meters.

**P.T.:** "I came from the Cross country World Championships in South Africa and was in the best shape of my career. I celebrated the record and then sometime later they told me the course was too short. They had never questioned the distance before. These are the kind of things that are very difficult for me to forget. Many times I put in a big effort, a special performance at a special place and something comes up. I stress this point because apart from that also when I ran the 59:06 in Portugal they said it was downhill but for many years they used to recognize the records of other people on the same route. Nevertheless, in all the years since 1998 nobody has even come close to my 59:17."

Running at the head of the field throughout the race, Paul Tergat totally dominated the 1998 Stramilano half-marathon in Milan. Setting off a burning pace, which he later qualified himself as excessive, he went trough the first kilometer mark in 2:38, the second in 2:39, the third in 2:42. "Perhaps I started off too fast. In fact, I paid for it at the end, otherwise I would have even been able to go under 59 minutes," Tergat admitted after the race.

His slowest time for any kilometer of the 21.097km race was 2:53 (for the 13th and last kilometer). And after all this he still covered the final 97 meters of the course in a blistering 14 seconds. His World Record of 59:17 knocked thirty seconds off the five-year-old mark of fellow Kenyan Moses Tanui (59:47, also in the Stramilano). Tergat had the record set firmly in his sights. "I was completely focused on the record. I wanted to break it, I thought of nothing else." And this year, the organizers had made sure that there was no repeat of the 1996 error. The course was measured and re-measured by IAAF official course measurer Jean François Delasalle.

# A DAY IN TERGAT'S LIFE

It was at the beginning of 1999 when Paul Tergat talked on the IAAF Web site about an ordinary day in his life. Here is what he had to say:

**P.T.:** *"What do you think life is like for a Kenyan who, thanks to his natural ability and especially to rigorous daily training, is able to reach the summit in world class athletics? Believe me, it is certainly not easy. Natural talent is not enough. I have seen young boys in Kenya who believe that they are better just because they come from Eldoret or Iten or Nakuru. They quickly learn that it is not so easy. To achieve something in sport, as in life, you have to work hard every day. Athletics is particularly unforgiving. In a typical day, athletics has a great significance but it is never the only thing to do. I will explain why. There are two periods in my training: when I train three times a day and when I only train twice. As you can imagine, this affects the rhythm of my day."*

*"In the phase of intensive training, my alarm goes off very early – at 5:30 in the morning. By 6 a.m. I am already outside. I have decided to live near Nairobi but outside the city. The town is called Ngong. To arrive at my home, you have to traverse Karen, where you will still find the house of the celebrated Danish author Baroness Karen Blixen and where everything – the school, the sport club, the hospital – resemble souvenirs. Since the beginning of December 1998 I have been in my new house. It is from here where I leave every morning to train. Every day I change my route. It is something stronger than me. And the hills of Ngong help me a lot in this respect. I know a dozen different training routes. Some kilometers from my home there is a military base where*

you can find a lot of Kenyan runners. Sometimes they come to run with me, but often I am alone. This doesn't bother me. I need to be surrounded by nature and to follow my own nature, to have variety and to never repeat myself.

For my first training session I run for about 40 minutes. After that, I immediately return home, take a shower, have breakfast and then rest. And while I drink my favorite Kenyan tea the telephone rings. It's inevitable. I speak to my associates, my coach, my manager, my family and to journalists. I don't actually have a lot of time because I need to be ready to leave for my second session at 10:00 a.m. This is the longest workout of the day – around 60 to 70 minutes – and the hardest. After training I return home for the same routine – shower, tea, rest. Then it is time for lunch with the family – my wife Monica and our two children Ronald and Harriet – and often another relative who is visiting. After the meal, I have a little time to spend with my kids – to listen to them, to play with them. It is a part of my life that is vital. The family is too important to slip away. Everything I do is for my wife and my children.

*The young Tergat family in 1999*

*Between 5 and 5:30 p.m. I leave for the third and final session of the day, which usually lasts around an hour. When that is over I come home for a traditional Kenyan meal, which could be ugali, cooked vegetables, rice, chicken and lamb. Afterwards, I may watch some television and chat with Monica and the kids before going to bed early. When I have only two sessions, I won't get up so early but I will be on the road by 9 a.m. Never later, because it is too hot. The second training session will be around 5 p.m. and last about an hour.*

*There is one thing that lately has irritated me a lot. And that is those fools who think and write that the Kenyan athletes have no soul but only care about money. It is really nonsense. I would ask any reasonably intelligent person – wouldn't you think it was normal for a man to care about his future? Take my example. People would like me to run everywhere. Yet, contrary to their desires, I carefully select my races, refusing many, and fix my precise objectives, as I have always done. And I have decided to invest most of the money I earn here in Kenya, so that my country can progress. I have been directing some business activities. For this reason I often leave Ngong during the week for my office in the big city.*

*Have you ever been to Kenya to see our wildlife? You should. It is an enriching experience. Consider the magnificent lions. During the night, they hunt. The male roars, the female makes the kill and the cubs watch. And then, it is time for them to feed. The male lion will not allow any other animal near the carcass, but if his cubs approach he will step aside and watch them eat. I, Paul Kibii Tergat, want always to watch my children eat with the knowledge that I have done everything I could for them."*

# TERGAT'S TIPS FOR THE HALF-MARATHON

The half-marathon is 21.097 kilometers long and an ideal intermediate stop on the way to the marathon, the classic, legendary distance and ultimate goal for most serious runners. But, for many runners, the half-marathon is an independent and attractive objective, in accordance with the motto: "half-marathon – full pleasure." The training for the half-marathon is not too costly.

Even if you have been running only 8 or 10 kilometers continuously so far with two or three training sessions a week, you will be able to participate in your first half-marathon in approximately four months. Please note: The training examples are a kind of a guiding principle. Be flexible with your personal program. Every runner has his or her strong and weak points that have to be considered when you draw up your program. Of course, the days can be changed, but you should never go for two successive intensive workouts.

Our program is split into three phases: The **starter stage** takes between 6 and 8 weeks and serves primarily to get used to the increased training days (4 sessions a week) and mileage. In the **foundation stage** (7-8 weeks), we increase the mileage once more and also the intensity. The **competition stage** contains the last 4 weeks before the half-marathon. The main target in this phase is to maintain the fitness level and to get used to the half-marathon pace.

It is recommended that you go for a test competition (or a fast run) of 10 kilometers, 3 to 4 weeks before the half-marathon. This way you can get used to the whole procedure of a competition and you can feel how your body reacts to the stress of a race.

# THE RIGHT PACE

The most exact way to find out the right pace for the different training runs and the competition are the performance tests (lactate or Conconi test). But even with a simple field test, you will know how fast you are supposed to run. Go for a 10km test run. Try to run the whole distance as fast and as regular as possible. If you need, for example 50 minutes for the 10 kilometers, it means the average of 5 minutes per kilometer corresponds to 100% of your strain intensity (or your anaerobic threshold). From this time, you are now able to calculate all the different running paces.

## TRAINING PACE

| | |
|---|---|
| Long jog | 5' + 30-50% = 6:30-7:30' |
| Easy run | 5' + 25% = 6:15' |
| Medium pace | 5' + 12% = 5:36' |
| Fast pace | 5' + 5% = 5:18' |
| Fartlek short | 5' – 3% to + 3% = 4:51 to 5:09' |
| Fartlek long | 5' – 3% to +12% = 4:51 to 5:36' |
| Half-marathon pace | 5' + 5-7% = 5:15 to 5:21' |

# TRAINING EXAMPLES

## STARTER STAGE

| | |
|---|---|
| Mon: | – |
| Tue: | 30-50' easy-medium pace, strength (strength exercises, rope-skipping) |
| Wed: | 10' warm-up/warm-down + coordination/accelerations |
| Thu: | – |
| Fri: | 30-50' easy-medium pace or cross training (aqua gym/deep water running, Nordic-walking, bike, swimming etc), strength |
| Sat: | – |
| Sun: | 50-80' easy run, begin with 50' in the first week and increase continuously |

## FOUNDATION STAGE

| | |
|---|---|
| Mon: | 10' warm-up/warm-down, 15' fartlek |
| Tue: | 40-60' easy run or cross training, strength |
| Wed: | – |
| Thu: | 10' warm-up/warm-down, 30-40' fast pace, strength/coordination |
| Fri: | – |
| Sat: | 70-110' long jog |
| Sun: | Recovery or alternations |

## COMPETITION STAGE

| | |
|---|---|
| Mon: | 10' warm-up/warm-down, 20' fartlek |
| Tue: | 30' easy run, strength/coordination |
| Wed: | – |
| Thu: | Variant 1: 20-30' fast pace; variant 2: 10' warm-up/warm-down, 4 x 5' half-marathon pace, 3' jogging in-between |
| Fri: | – |
| Sat: | 80-120' long jog (last 2 weeks before the half-marathon not more than 100') |
| Sun: | Recovery or alternations |

## COMPETITION WEEK

| | |
|---|---|
| Mo: | – |
| Tue: | 15' fartlek |
| Wed: | 30-40' easy run |
| Thu: | – |
| Fri: | 30' easy run, 5 accelerations |
| Sat: | **HALF-MARATHON** |

*Integrate stretching (5-7 exercises, 15 min in total) at least two times a week in your training.*

**Alternations:**
Half or two-thirds of the time is used with running, followed by cross training sports. At the end again at least 15 min running.

**Coordination:**
Accelerations and "running school" are recommended once or twice a week before a fast workout (fast pace, fartlek).

**Cross training:**
Aqua gym/deep water running, Nordic-walking, bike, swimming, etc.

**Recovery:**
At least once a week, recovery is recommended. Sauna, massage or a bath is especially suitable.

# WHAT IS A FARTLEK?

This kind of training has its origin in Scandinavia and means playing with the various running paces. Depending on the pace, the endurance, the speed and up to a certain level even the strength will improve. In the Swedish fartlek, you change the pace in a playful manner according to the profile of the roads or the open country. In the Polish fartlek, the distances and the times are fixed, for example: 30''/ 60''/ 90''/ 2'/ 3'/ 90''/ 60''/ 30'' fast with the same jogging intervals in-between.

*Sydney 2000: After 10,000 meters there where only nine hundreth of a second between the two big rivals. The gold belonged to Gebrselassie*

# THE ETERNAL DUELS WITH HAILE

For many years, Paul Tergat had the same program: cross country, road (six-time winner in the Stramilano half-marathon) and then the track. Some critics wondered if it wouldn't have been better instead of running on the road to go back to Kenya after the cross country season, to recover for a short time and then concentrate on preparing for the track, the way Haile Gebrselassie and other Ethiopians usually did. Tergat doesn't like the question at all. Indeed, he was and is the only athlete of the modern times who was able to win the cross country World Championships and break World Records on the road and on the track.

**P.T.:** *"For me, I think it was the right thing to do, because I loved cross country, but I liked the road and the track, too. I wanted to prove that I could run very fast on all surfaces. It is true, Haile won four World and two Olympic titles on the track and four indoors and he won the half-marathon title in 2001, but I am very happy for what I have achieved. We should not forget: In 1997, I won my third world title in cross country, three weeks later the Stramilano for the fourth time and five months later I was still, and again in my top shape when I broke the 10,000m World Record in Brussels. Running cross and on the road always gave me a lot of confidence for the track season."*

Who could have believed it, but after Haile Gebrselassie won the 3,000m at the Van Damme Memorial in Brussels on August 22, 1997, he lost both his World Records! Daniel Komen took the 5,000m in 12:39,74 and Paul Tergat the 10,000m in 26:27,85. William Kalya led the leading group in the 10k at 5,000m. When Salah Hissou, who had set a World Record in the same stadium the previous year, dropped back from 7km, it was down to Paul Koech and Tergat. Tergat ran the second half in an astonishing 13:09,8 – 20 years earlier this would have been a World Record at 5,000m! Henry Rono, the great Kenyan who broke four World Records in 1978 at 3,000m, 5,000m, 10,000m and 3,000m steeplechase within 65 days was the first runner to finish the twelve and a half laps under 13:10 min.

Paul Koech was more than 8 seconds behind in 26:36,26 but was still running faster than the pre-season World Record. Koech had played a very important role in Tergat's career. So many times the Army captain from Nakuru where there is the lake with the famous flamingos, took care of a fast pace and helped his friend to unfold his potential. He always was extremely solid, running a high speed but unfortunately he didn't have a kick. So this extraordinary athlete managed to win only one international title: at the World Half-marathon Championship 1998 in Switzerland and – with seven participations – only one individual silver at the World Cross country Championships, earlier in the same year at Marrakesh. Paul Koech later suffered a stubborn knee injury but still ran the marathon in 2:07,07 (2nd in Chicago 2003).

*Daniel Komen and Paul Tergat in the outfit of the national team*

In the days before the Van Damme Memorial, the newspapers concentrated much more on Salah Hissou than Tergat. Hardly anybody seemed to take note of his strong showing August 6 at the World Championships in Athens (second behind Gebrselassie who ran the last lap in 55.2 seconds) and above all his brilliant 5000m race seven days later at the Weltklasse in Zürich where he came third at 12:49,87, just eight seconds off Gebrselassie who had established a new World Record – the one he lost now in Brussels to Komen.

**BRUSSELS:**

| | | |
|---|---|---|
| 1,000m | 2:40,6 | |
| 2,000m | 5:21,0 | (2:40,4) |
| 3,000m | 8:00,6 | (2:39,6) |
| 4,000m | 10:37,2 | (2:36,6) |
| 5,000m | 13:18,0 | (2:40,8) |
| 6,000m | 15:58,2 | (2:40,2) |
| 7,000m | 18:37,8 | (2:39,6) |
| 8,000m | 21:15,7 | (2:37,9) |
| 9,000m | 23:52,1 | (2:36,4) |
| 10,000m | 26:27,85 | (2:35,7) |

(second half: 13:09,8, last 3,000m: 7:50)

*Federico Rosa, who works as an athletes' representative in his father's company, with Tergat and other runners in St. Moritz*

Paul Tergat had prepared for the August events in the Swiss holiday resort of St. Moritz where the track is 1,860m above sea level and where you can run at an altitude of 2,500m. In the course of the years, St. Moritz has become the ultimate place to prepare the second half of the season for most of the world's best middle and long distance runners. Tergat was at St. Moritz with his coach, Dr. Rosa, and some other athletes from the Fila "stable" during a four weeks period. To Athens, Zurich and Brussels, he traveled directly from St. Moritz.

The training in the Swiss mountains was very intense, both in quality and quantity. He covered about 210km a week and on a daily basis he underwent a more or less demanding workout – Rosa calls it a "technical training session." In specific, three of these technical trainings were done on the track and three on the grass. On the track, we talk about intervals; on the grass, mostly diagonals (15 x 180-200 meters on a polo field). Three examples of the track sessions he did in St. Moritz:

- 25x 400m in 56" with 1'15" recovery

- 10x 1000m, the first one in 2'33",
  the last one in 2'30" with 1'30" recovery

- 1x 3000m in 8'10" with 2' recovery,
  followed by 2x 2000m in 5'15" with 2' recovery

Coach Gabriele Rosa: "What is even more noticeable: these hard workouts are supposed to be carried out at sea level while Paul performed them at 1,860 meters above." Rosa attaches great importance to the fact that only Africans who are used to the high altitude and who are in a very good shape could do this kind of training. He admits that with Moses Tanui, his first world-class athlete, he was not so courageous when it came to the training programs. "I was afraid to push him for his 10,000m training. When I started with Kenyan athletes, I came with the mentality and the knowledge of somebody who used to coach Europeans. Only after some time I realized that they are able to cope with a much tougher training regime.

Otherwise, Moses Tanui could have run considerably faster than the 27:18 he did in 1993 in Brussels. With Tergat's program, he could have run easily below 27 minutes. He was definitely more talented than Yobes Ondieki who was to be the first man to break the 27-minute barrier in 1993."

**P.T.:** *"The World Record in Brussels was the climax of my career so far. World Championships and Olympic games are only titles. I always dreamed that on one day at one distance I could be able to run faster than any human before me. A World Record is the greatest an athlete can achieve."*

In later years Tergat intended to attack the record two more times: in Stockholm and Brussels 1999. But now he didn't find the right pacesetters anymore. Paul Koech was out with an injury. Others had turned against him and his coach Gabriele Rosa who by now had a large group of very strong runners, especially in marathon. And this was something not everybody liked. Some agents preferred when their athletes paced for an Ethiopian than for Tergat. This was a development Tergat didn't understand, "because it is not only the one who breaks the record who gets a certain amount from the organizers but also the pacemakers." And he adds: "Today people run for Adidas, Nike, Fila or Puma and not for Kenya anymore."

*Gabriele Rosa, Tergat and Paul Koech at the Olympics 1996 in Atlanta. Here is where the plans were hatched*

## GEBRSELASSIE VS. TERGAT AT 10.000M

| 1995 | WCh Gothenburg: | 1. Gebrselassie 27:12,95 |
| | | 3. Tergat 27:14,70 |

| 1996 | Olympics Atlanta: | 1. Gebrselassie 27:07,34 |
| | | 2. Tergat 27:08,17 |

| 1997 | WCh Athens: | 1. Gebrselassie 27:24,58 |
| | | 2. Tergat 27:25,62 |

| 1999 | WCh Seville: | 1. Gebrselassie 27:57,27 |
| | | 2. Tergat 27:58,56 |

| 2000 | Olympics Sydney: | 1. Gebrselassie 27:18,20 |
| | | 2. Tergat 27:18,29 |

In cross country, Haile Gebrselassie managed to win only one bronze medal as a senior at the World Championships, 1994 in Budapest. In 1995, he was fourth and in 1996 fifth. But when it comes to the track, the great Ethiopian was the dominating long distance runner for one decade.

*Pictures from 1996: in the Olympic village with the Kenyan flag and together with his parents back in Kenya*

When Paul Tergat ran his last race on the track before shifting to the marathon, in the Olympic final 2000 in Sydney, it seems he could finally win the gold medal he would have so richly deserved after coming second to Gebrselassie three times in a row. But again the Ethiopian snatched the gold medal away from him. It was the closest finish in Olympic history: Only nine hundreths of a second seperated the two rivals – after 10,000m not even half a meter! On September 25, Tergat was in the shape of his life. But then, 300 meters before the finish line, Gebrselassie's teammate Assefa Mezegebu blocked him, Tergat had to slow down and go around Mezegebu before he could launch his attack. On the last few meters, he could not resist Gebrselassie anymore. Maybe he should have waited until the last bend for his attack – after the battle you are always wiser.

Again he was "only" second, the same as four years ago when the Kenyan team had tried to run down the Ethiopians with a deadly pace. After a slow first half in 13:55,22 Paul Koech had made the first big move and covered the 6th kilometer in 2:40,44, Josephat Machuka the 7th in 2:42,88 and Koech the 8th in 2:43,62, at which point six Africans remained in contention. Then Tergat took off with a 29-second 200, with only Gebrselassie able to respond. The 9th kilometer took 2:33,90 and the final one 2:31,46, with Tergat leading until the bell. Tergat and Gebrselassie had run the second half in about 13:11,6 and the last 2000m in 5:05.
Once more, Gebrselassie proved his special ability to hang on by a supreme effort and squeeze him like a lemon until the last drop. Let's not forget: For a tall man like Tergat (1,82m), it is always more difficult to accelerate and sprint than for a shorter athlete (Gebrselassie measures 1,64m), even if he worked a lot and had success over the years to improve his final speed.

**P.T.:** *"I think it was bad luck, especially in Sydney. If it is one second you have to accept that the other one was stronger. But a few hundreths – this is nothing. Of course some people even in my surroundings speculate that the Ethiopians may use a kind of drugs, but me I always denied this. I accept that Haile was luckier than me when it came to the Olympics. I am not bitter. I was not given. But I am not the only one. Wilson Kipketer was dominating the 800 meters for a decade, but never won an Olympic gold. Neither did Moses Kiptanui, the king of steeplechase. This is sport. I respect Haile very much for what he has achieved. He is a great champion – and a great friend of mine. I was even at his home in Addis. I have a lot of kindly customs. I knowthat he was always training very, very hard, maybe even harder than me. Haile is the one who was forcing me to do more. He was a challenge over all the years since I started running on the top level. Always when we met it was a real fight. And he kept me motivated. I owe a lot to him. I believe that without him I could never have done what I did as a runner. But I am certain that on the other hand he too benefited from our rivalry."*

There was another event when Tergat finished second close to Gebrselassie. Tergat missed a huge pay check and fame outside athletics for the lead role in the Hollywood sports blockbuster *Endurance* for failing to win the 1996 Atlanta Olympics in 10,000 meters gold. When the directors decided to do the movie about a simple African boy who overcame heavy odds to conquer the world, they found themselves in a dilemma over whom to select for the lead character.

Tergat had just won his second World Cross country title, Gebrselassie was the reigning World Champion at 10,000m and the new star on the track since the 1992 World Junior Championships where he spiked Josphat Machuka unintentionally and for this reason earned a punch from the Kenyan at the finish line.

The majority settled on Tergat. They found him and his physique fitted perfectly to their script. The country with its famed wildlife and landscape provided the perfect settings for *Endurance*.

But finally they reached the consensus of picking their hero from the winner of the Olympics in Atlanta. The rest is history.

*Tergat with his wife Monica and the two daughters Harriet (left) and Gloria after arriving from Sydney*

*Happy and proud after finishing his first marathon 2001 in London*

# Chapter 6

# NEW CHALLENGE: MARATHON

The 10,000m final at the Olympics in Sydney was Tergat's last race on the track. Now he had transformed into a marathon runner. He had offers from many race organizers to make his debut marathon in their cities, but he choose London because he wanted a fast, flat course and enthusiastic spectators and he believed he would get all of this in the British capital. Dave Bedford, the London race director, had been chasing after Tergat's signature for 18 months. Tergat's one-year deal with the Flora London Marathon was worth $ 300,000 US, the most lucrative in the history of road running.

**P.T.:** *"I always liked to break into new grounds. I never wanted only to compete. I always wanted something special. After Sydney I didn't have a motivation on the track anymore. So it was high time for me to shift to the marathon. When I decided to run the marathon some people told me I would be too tall, I could never do it. I listened to what they said but I didn't take it seriously. I never believe something is impossible. Only when I try I know if it is possible or not."*

Tergat was motivated and enthusiastic when he started the marathon preparation at the beginning of December 2000. He had to adapt his training slowly. Indeed, he could not change everything from one day to another. At that point, his longest runs were around 22 kilometers. Then he increased his weekly long run gradually, first to 25, then to 30 and finally to 38 kilometers or in other words: up to 2 hours 10, 2 hours 20. As a 10,000m runner, he used to do speed-work for half an hour, but now it was up to one hour with intervals, fartleks. Until the end of February, Tergat did the training from his home at Ngong outside Nairobi. Then he moved to Eldoret where athletes, such as Moses Tanui, Elijah Lagat, Joshua Chelang'a, Simon Biwott and Japhet Kosgei, practiced for their spring marathons in and around Kaptagat forest, with two sessions a day, often 25 kilometers in the morning and another 15 in the afternoon, and on Sundays they did the long run of 30 to 38km. All in all, he covered between 260 and 280 kilometers a week during the two most intensive months. The last month before the marathon there were a lot of shorter, faster sessions of 12 or 15km, fartlek and track workouts for regaining speed. Tergat admitted it was the hardest training he had ever done in his career. It was the only time he prepared at Kaptagat. Later, he always had his training base at home. "My body is not used to an altitude of 2,300m above sea level, the area around Ngong is only 1,700 or 1,800 meters high. The training at Kaptagat was exhausting. Every evening I was very, very tired."

*At the burial of Tergat's father Kipkuna Tuiotek in December 2000: in the foreground the three widows (Tergat's mother on the right), behind with Tergat: the two white men Jürg Wirz and Federico Rosa*

The "day of days" was April 22. It was the most eagerly awaited debut in marathon history. "Whether I win or lose, I will have ventured into the unknown," Tergat said. Indeed, only such pragmatism could have endeared him to millions of fans. It is what underscores his approach to life, on and off the track. The race progressed for a long time according to the expectation of the experts. After the 35km mark, the Moroccan Abdelkader El Mouaziz tried once again to escape and now it was only Tergat who was able to follow him. But not for long. When the marathon entered its decisive stage, Tergat lost contact. Later, he admitted that he expected Antonio Pinto to come from behind so that they could chase El Mouaziz together. But the Portuguese was not able to repeat the effort from the previous year, and so Tergat crossed the finish line one minute behind the Moroccan.

**P.T.:** *"I was expecting more pain in my first marathon, more confusion also. I was very worried I might have to stop on the last few kilometers. Coming second to El Mouaziz in a time of 2:08 was very much okay because deep in my mind I just wanted to finish. After the race, I felt a lot of pain in my legs, something I had never experienced before in my whole life. Somebody had to remove my shoes. I could hardly walk. I thought I was the only one having these problems. Later, I realized that even the last one finishing a marathon has paining legs."*

Paul Tergat had a good start to his new career but it was not the bombshell many observers expected. He decided to grow slowly into the new challenge, the new distance and tactics. It took two and a half years and four more marathons before he was ready to attack the World Record in Berlin. In his second marathon, in early October in Chicago, Tergat had to learn a new lesson: Never trust a pacemaker! He went into the race with a lot of hope and confidence, but nobody had told him that in a marathon a pacemaker is allowed to finish the race. He feels he was tricked and conned. He took care of all the other people and so it happened that his countryman Ben Kimondiu, the man wearing the bib with the word "pace" was winning the race. Yet, after this, Kimondiu was not seen anymore. "It is easy to run fast when you are a pacemaker, but when you have to run your own race, it is a completely different story. Then you have to cope a lot of pressure," Tergat commented, confessing it was a shock and a disappointment.

*Chicago Marathon 2001*

In spring 2002 Paul Tergat came again to London. Now he felt already like a real marathon runner. But again the lack of experience cost him his first marathon victory. It was at the last drinking station when he slowed down and took his water. Khalid Khannouchi used this moment in a very smart manner for the decisive attack and crossed the line in a new world best of 2:05:38. Tergat was stunned: To run 2:05:48 and not win the race was unbelievable for him. What could he say? Was he not able to win? At the same time, it gave him another push and a lot of confidence that he would be able to attack the World Record himself very soon. This was also the race Haile Gebrselassie finished in third position (2:06:35) but decided nevertheless to continue as a track runner until the 2004 Olympics.

In October 2002, Tergat was running for the second time in Chicago. Although he ran again a very fast time with 2:06:18, at the end of the year position six in the world list, he only finished fourth. Khannouchi was the clear winner but the second-place Kenyan Daniel Njenga was just two seconds ahead of Tergat.

**P.T.:** *"First I didn't want to run in Chicago. I almost withdrew because of my brother Francis who was very sick at that time. Before the race I went to see him in the hospital. The doctors told me there was nothing they could do for him anymore. He had liver cancer that was diagnosed in September 2001. He was put on several rounds of chemotherapy of which the doctors hoped to stop the tumor and make it possible for a surgery to be done. This unfortunately failed, thus the cancer spread to the bones. I knew after the race I would take him back to Kenya.*

*I was the one to decide. I couldn't let him die in the USA whereas the family was at home. When I was in Chicago I sent for his wife and the two children. On the way to Nairobi we had to fly in first class because he was not able to sit anymore. Two weeks later he passed away in Nairobi Hospital. When I came to Chicago I was deeply distressed because Francis was the brother who was the closest to me, he was the one who followed me.*

*I was running a race where my mind was not there. I could not concentrate on the marathon at all but I didn't tell the organizers or the media about my personal problems. I always prefer keeping my private life for my own. Even the fatally ill Francis didn't want me to talk about it. He was a very strong guy. The World Record I did in Berlin I did it in his honor."*

In London in 2003, Tergat had a lot of difficulties, including stomach problems and vomiting almost from the beginning. Nevertheless, he managed to complete the race in 2:07:58. It was the closest finish in the history of the Flora London Marathon with six runners within seven seconds: Sydney Olympic Champion Gezahegne Abera from Ethiopia in front of Stefano Baldini, the Italian who would become the Olympic winner four years later, Joseph Ngolepus (KEN), Tergat, Samson Ramadhani (TAN) and the winner from the previous year, El Mouaziz.

After these five marathons, Tergat knew he was completely inside the marathon. Now he was ready for his master. It was only a question of the right time, the right course, the right weather and the right form.

*In June 2000 the family was complete: Paul and Monica Tergat, Ronald, Harriet and little Gloria*

# TERGAT'S TRAINING FOR LONDON 2002

| WEEK 1 | MORNING | AFTERNOON |
|---|---|---|
| January 14 (Mon): | 1h 10' | 1h |
| January 15 (Tue): | 35km | 1h |
| January 16 (Wed) | 1h 15' | 1h |
| January 17 (Thu): | 1h 15' | recover |
| January 18 (Fri): | 1h 10' | 1h |
| January 19 (Sat): | 30' + 20x 1' fast, 1' slow | 1h |
| January 20 (Sun): | 1h 10' | 30' + 15 diagonals (180-200m) |

| WEEK 2 | MORNING | AFTERNOON |
|---|---|---|
| January 21 (Mon): | 1h 10' | 1h |
| January 22 (Tue): | 30km | recover |
| January 23 (Wed): | 1h 10' | 1h |
| January 24 (Thu): | 30' + 8x 1,000m (2'47'') rec. 1'30'' + 5x 400m (60'') rec. 1'50'' | 1h |
| January 25 (Fri): | 1h 10' | 1h |
| January 26 (Sat): | 1h 15' | 30' + 15 diagonals (180-200m) |
| January 27 (Sun): | 30km | recover |

## WEEK 3

| | MORNING | AFTERNOON |
|---|---|---|
| January 28 (Mon): | 1h 15' | 1h |
| January 29 (Tue): | 30' + 25x 1' fast, 1' slow | 1h |
| January 30 (Wed): | 1h 20' | 1h |
| January 31 (Thu): | 1h 10' | 1h |
| February 1 (Fri): | 30km | recover |
| February 2 (Sat): | 1h 10' | 1h |
| February 3 (Sun): | 1h 15' | 1h |

## WEEK 4

| | MORNING | AFTERNOON |
|---|---|---|
| February 4 (Mon): | 30' + 10x 1,000m (2'45'') rec. 1'30'' | 1h |
| February 5 (Tue): | 1h 10' | 1h |
| February 6 (Wed): | 1h 15' | 1h |
| February 7 (Thu): | 35km | recover |
| February 8 (Fri): | 1h 10' | 1h |
| February 9 (Sat): | 1h 10' | 1h |
| February 10 (Sun): | 30' + 20x 1' fast, 1' slow | 1h |

| WEEK 5 | MORNING | AFTERNOON |
|---|---|---|
| February 11 (Mon): | 1h 10' | 1h |
| February 12 (Tue): | 1h 15' | 1h |
| February 13 (Wed): | 30km | recover |
| February 14 (Thu): | 1h 10' | 1h |
| February 15 (Fri): | 1h 15' | 1h |
| February 16 (Sat): | 30' + 4x 2,000m (5'42''-5'45'') rec. 2' + 2x 1,000m (2'45'') rec. 1'30'' | 1h |
| February 17 (Sun): | 1h 10' | 1h |

| WEEK 6 | MORNING | AFTERNOON |
|---|---|---|
| February 18 (Mon): | 1h 10' | 1h |
| February 19 (Tue): | travel | |
| February 20 (Wed): | 1h 10' | 1h |
| February 21 (Thu): | 1h | 50' |
| February 22 (Fri) | 50' | 40' |
| February 23 (Sat) | 30' | recover |
| February 24 (Sun): | 10km Puerto Rico | |

## WEEK 7

| | MORNING | AFTERNOON |
|---|---|---|
| February 25 (Mon): | travel | |
| February 26 (Tue): | 1h 10' | 1h |
| February 27 (Wed): | 1h 15' | 1h |
| February 28 (Thu): | 35km | recover |
| March 1 (Fri): | 1h 10' | 1h |
| March 2 (Sat): | 30' + 25x 1' fast, 1' slow | 1h |
| March 3 (Sun): | 1h 10' | 1h |

## WEEK 8

| | MORNING | AFTERNOON |
|---|---|---|
| March 4 (Mon): | 30' + 3x 3,000m (8'40''-8'45'') + 2x 1,000m (2'45'') rec. 1'30'' | 1h |
| March 5 (Tue): | 1h 10' | 1h |
| March 6 (Wed): | 1h 10' | 1h |
| March 7 (Thu): | 30km | recover |
| March 8 (Fri): | 1h 10' | 1h |
| March 9 (Sat): | 40' + 20x 1' fast, 1' slow | 1h |
| March 10 (Sun): | 1h 10 | 1h |

## WEEK 9

| | MORNING | AFTERNOON |
|---|---|---|
| March 11 (Mon): | 30' + 12x 1,000m (2'45'') rec. 1'30'' | 1h |
| March 12 (Tue): | 1h 10' | 1h |
| March 13 (Wed): | 38km | recover |
| March 14 (Thu): | 1h 10' | 1h |
| March 15 (Fri): | 40' + 20x 1' fast, 1' slow | 1h |
| March 16 (Sat): | 1h 10' | 1h |
| March 17 (Sun): | 1h 10' | 1h |

## WEEK 10

| | MORNING | AFTERNOON |
|---|---|---|
| March 18 (Mon): | 30' + 10x 1,000m (2'45'') rec. 1'30'' | 1h |
| March 19 (Tue): | 1h 10' | 1h |
| March 20 (Wed): | 1h 10' | 1h |
| March 21 (Thu): | travel | |
| March 22 (Fri): | 1h | 50' |
| March 23 (Sat): | 30' | recover |
| March 24 (Sun): | Lisbon half-marathon | |

## WEEK 11

| | MORNING | AFTERNOON |
|---|---|---|
| March 25 (Mon): | travel | |
| March 26 (Tue): | 1h 10' | 1h |
| March 27 (Wed): | 35km | recover |
| March 28 (Thu): | 1h 10' | 1h |
| March 29 (Fri): | 40' + 25x 1' fast, 1' slow | 1h |
| March 30 (Sat): | 1h 10' | 1h |
| March 31 (Sun): | 1h 10' | 1h |

## WEEK 12

| | MORNING | AFTERNOON |
|---|---|---|
| April 1 (Mon): | 30' + 5x 2,000m (5'42''-5:45'') rec 2' + 2x 1,000m (2'45'') rec 1'30'' | 1h |
| April 2 (Tue): | 1h 10' | 1h |
| April 3 (Wed): | 25km | recover |
| April 4 (Thu): | 1h 10' | 1h |
| April 5 (Fri): | 40' + 20x 1' fast, 1' slow | 1h |
| April 6 (Sat): | 1h 10' | 1h |
| April 7 (Sun): | 30' + 2x 5,000m (14'10''-14'15'') rec 2' + 2x1,000m (2'45'') rec 1'30'' | 1h |

| | MORNING | AFTERNOON |
|---|---|---|
| April 8 (Mon): | 1h 10' | 30' + 15 diagonals (180-200m) |
| April 9 (Tue): | travel | |
| April 10 (Wed): | 30' + 15 diagonals (180-200m) | 40' |
| April 11 (Thu): | 50' | 40' |
| April 12 (Fri): | 50' | 40' |
| April 13 (Sat): | recover | recover |
| April 14 (Sun): | 2nd London Marathon 2:05:48 | |

**Remarks:** The training in the morning (around 1h 10') is always between medium and fast, the afternoon training (usually 1h) is between slow and medium. The long runs (30-38km) are not slow at all. Tergat's home area (Ngong) where he does his marathon training is rather hilly! The intervals (400m, 1,000m, 2,000m and 3,000m repetitions) are run on the track.

When he prepared for the World Record in Berlin, he used the same program but he extended his longest run to 45km (2h29' on a hilly course).

In preparation for the Olympics in Athens, he did at least one morning run a week over 1h 10' uphill, and he increased the mileage again slightly. He covered up to 300km a week.

TERGAT'S TIPS FOR THE MARATHON

Marathon is the absolute challenge. It is a passion. It is the mother of all battles. When you go for a marathon, you need to be ready. Everything has to be right. The physical and mental preparation, the food you were eating in the days and hours before, the drinks you are taking, the pace you choose... It doesn't matter if you are going to walk, to jog or if you are running as fast as you can. At one point, the body is changing and the marathon is starting to eat you. This is the deciding moment – the moment when the whole body is crying and wants to stop and only your mind keeps you going. Maybe the shoe is causing a problem and pinching you, maybe you feel a twitch in your left knee... Don't worry: Even the best runners have these kinds of problems!

But it is not the pain that disturbs you most. It is the self-pity. The mind is becoming exhausted and weak. This is the marathon! Now you have to be strong – and you will, because this is what you have prepared for months or even years. The better your endurance, the better you will handle the problems on the last part of the race.

The readiness in a marathon depends a lot on the mental preparation. I believe in any kind of sport the mental power is at least 50 percent of a performance. In my case, I would say only one quarter is the physical aspect, three quarters concern the mental part. When you are running a marathon, you fight with so many things: with the competitors or your personal weaknesses, the weather and the distance. The 42.195 kilometers is a challenge for everybody, even if you are the World Record holder in the half-marathon. After finishing a marathon even I have sore muscles. I have the problem of walking, going down stairs.

At the start of the marathon, you have to believe in yourself. You have to believe in your training. You have to believe in your ability. This belief makes the difference between two athletes who were following the same training program. I think the mental sphere is also a question of the personality. Some of us can bear more pain or suffering than others.

A marathon is the crowning moment in the life of a runner. Sooner or later every serious runner will reach the point when he or she wants to plunge into this ultimate adventure. Marathon is definitely a new dimension. It is one of the biggest challenges our world has to offer. For sure, you have seen yourself these pitiful creatures that are dragging their bodies over the last kilometers of a marathon, almost collapsing. We want to save you from passing through the same experiences. For you the first marathon is supposed to become a positive experience. If you follow our tips and program you will be prepared when the big day arrives!

As in the case of the half-marathon the training program for the marathon is divided in three phases: *the starter stage (6-8 weeks), the foundation stage (7-8 weeks) and the competition stage (approximately 5 weeks)*. All in all you should have four, better five months of preparation, provided you are already able to run continuously between 1:30 and 2 hours.

# TRAINING EXAMPLES

**Your goal:** running the marathon under 3 hours – the ultimate target for most of the serious "amateurs." If you have been running the half-marathon distance already for some years and your personal best is between 1:20 and 1:25h you can do it. Mileage per week: 80-100km, 6 trainings a week.

## STARTER STAGE

| | |
|---|---|
| Mon: | 15km easy run, strength (strength exercises, rope-skipping) |
| Tue: | – |
| Wed: | 20km easy run |
| Thu: | 15km medium pace, strength |
| Fri: | 12km easy run |
| Sat: | cross training (aqua gym/deep water running, Nordic-walking, bike, swimming, etc.) |
| Sun: | 100-120' long jog |

## FOUNDATION STAGE

| | |
|---|---|
| Mon: | 15km easy run |
| Tue: | – |
| Wed: | Variant 1: 10' warm-up/warm-down, 15km medium-fast pace; variant 2: 10' warm-up/ warm-down, 3x 20' marathon pace, 3' jogging in-between |
| Thu: | 15-20km easy run |

| Fri: | 15km easy run, last 3 km medium-fast, coordination |
|------|-----|
| Sat: | 15km easy run, strength |
| Sun: | general aerobic endurance (120-180' long jog or 3-4h alternations) or specific aerobic endurance (variant 1: 10' warm-up/warm-down, fartlek 4x 10' (also hills), 3-5' jogging in-between); variant 2: 10' warm-up/warm-down, fartlek 3x (10' fast, 3' slow, 5' fast, 2' slow, 2' fast, 4' slow); variant 3: race (not longer than 25km) |

## COMPETITION STAGE

| Mon: | 15-20km easy run, last 3km marathon pace, strength, coordination |
|------|-----|
| Tue: | – or cross training (aqua gym/deep water running, Nordic-walking, bike, swimming, etc.) |
| Wed: | 15km easy run |
| Thu: | Variant 1: 10' warm-up/warm-down 3x 25' marathon pace, 3' jogging in-between; variant 2: 10' warm-up/warm-down, fartlek 3x (12' fast, 4' slow, 6' fast, 3' slow), variant 3: 10' warm-up/warm-down, 40' fartlek |
| Fri: | 20km easy run |
| Sat: | – or 15km medium pace |
| Sun: | 120-150' long jog or 2-4h alternations |

**Your goal:** under 4 hours. Mileage per week: 50-70km, 4-5 trainings.

## STARTER STAGE

| | |
|---|---|
| Mon: | 10km easy run, strength (strength exercises, rope-skipping) |
| Tue: | – |
| Wed: | 15-18km easy run |
| Thu: | 10-12km medium pace, strength |
| Fri: | – |
| Sat: | Cross training |
| Sun: | 90-120' long jog |

## FOUNDATION STAGE

| | |
|---|---|
| Mon: | 10-12km easy run |
| Tue: | – |
| Wed: | Variant 1: 10' warm-up/warm-down, 10-15km medium-fast pace; variant 2: 10' warm-up/warm-down, 3x 15 min marathon pace, 3' jogging in-between |
| Thu: | 8-10km easy run, strength, coordination |
| Fri: | – |
| Sat: | 10-15km easy run |
| Sun: | General aerobic endurance (120-180' long jog or 3-4 h alternations) or specific aerobic endurance;<br>Variant 1: 10' warm-up/warm-down, fartlek |

5x 5' (also hills), 3-5' jogging in-between;
Variant 2: 10' warm-up/warm-down, fartlek 3x (8' fast, 3' slow, 4' fast, 2' slow, 2' fast, 4' slow);
Variant 3: race (not longer than half-marathon)

## COMPETITION STAGE

| | |
|---|---|
| Mon: | 15km easy run, last 1-2km marathon pace, strength |
| Tue: | – |
| Wed: | Cross training |
| Thu: | 10km easy run |
| Fri: | Variant 1: 10' warm-up/warm-down, 3x 20' marathon pace, 3' jogging in-between; Variant 2: 10' warm-up/warm-down, fartlek 3x (10' fast, 3 min slow, 5' fast, 2' slow); Variant 3: 10' warm-up/warm-down, 30' fartlek |
| Sat: | – |
| Sun: | 105-150' long jog or 2-4h alternations |

**Your goal:** Finisher. Mileage per week: 30-50km, 3-4 trainings.

## STARTER STAGE

| | |
|---|---|
| Mon: | 30-45' easy run, strength (strength exercises, rope-skipping) |
| Tue: | – |
| Wed: | 30-45' easy run |
| Thu: | – |
| Fri: | Cross training, strength |
| Sat: | Easy run, begin with 60min and increase every week by 5', 5' walking every 5km or 30'; or 80-120' Nordic-walking |
| Sun: | – |

## FOUNDATION STAGE

| | |
|---|---|
| Mon: | 30-60' easy run, strength |
| Tue: | – |
| Wed: | Variant 1: 10' warm-up/warm-down, 20-30' medium-fast pace;<br>Variant 2: 10' warm-up/warm-down, 15-15' marathon pace;<br>Variant 3: 10' warm-up/warm-down, 15' fartlek |
| Thu: | – |
| Fri: | Cross training, strength |
| Sat: | Easy run, begin with 90' and increase every week by 5-10', 3' walking every 30'; or 90-150' Nordic-walking; or 2-3h alternations; or race (10km-half-marathon) |
| Sun: | – |

| | |
|---|---|
| Mon: | 30-60' easy run, strength, coordination |
| Tue: | – |
| Wed: | Variant 1: 10' warm-up/warm-down, 30-45' medium-fast pace;<br>Variant 2: 10' warm-up/warm-down, 3x 10-15' marathon pace, 3' jogging in-between |
| Thu: | – |
| Fri: | 30-45' easy run, strength |
| Sat: | 90-150' easy run (walking in-between); or 120-180' Nordic-walking (not later than 2 weeks before the marathon); or 2-4 h alternations |
| Sun: | – |

## MARATHON WEEK

| | |
|---|---|
| Mon: | – |
| Tue: | Variant 1: 10' warm-up/warm-down, fartlek 3x 10' marathon pace, 5' jogging in-between; variant 2: 10' warm-up/warm-down, fartlek 5-1-1-1-1-1 min fast, 5-1-1-1-1 min slow |
| Wed: | 30-40' easy run |
| Thu: | – |
| Fri: | – |
| Sat: | 30' easy run, 5 accelerations |
| Sun: | **MARATHON** |

*Integrate stretching (5-7 exercises, 15 min in total) at least two times a week in your training.*

**Alternations:** Half or two thirds of the time is used with running, followed by a cross training sport. At the end again, at least 15min running.

**Coordination:** Accelerations and "running school" are recommended once or twice a week before a fast workout (fast pace, fartlek).

**Cross training:** Bike, inline skating, swimming, aqua gym/deep water running, Nordic-walking, cross country skiing, etc.

**Recovery:** At least once a week recovery is recommended. Sauna, massage or a bath is especially suitable.

## THE RIGHT MARATHON PACE

Many marathon newcomers are making the same mistake: They zoom off like the fire brigade and they nearly collapse on the second part of the race. In other spheres of life, it might be advisable to get in some reserves but in a marathon, this tactic is deadly. The best marathon runners in the world manage to run at a constant time; some are even faster on the second half. When Tergat broke the World Record in Berlin, he passed the 21.1 kilometer mark in 63 minutes and ran the second half in 61:55!

What is the right marathon pace? We are going to present to you a simple formula. The only figure you need for the calculation is your half-marathon time. And this is how it goes: Let's say your half-marathon time is 1:45h = 5min/km. Your realistic marathon time: half-marathon + 10% = 5:30min/km or 3:51h marathon time respectively.

**In the luggage:**

- 2 pairs of shoes
- Spare shoe lace
- At least 4 pairs of socks
- Shorts and singlet
- T-shirt and shirt with long sleeves
- Short and long tights
- Rain jacket
- Cap and gloves
- Sun cream and sun glasses
- Old tracksuit or dustbin liner for keeping warm at the start
- Spare underwear
- Probably drink belt
- Toiletries, towel
- Stop watch
- Plaster, foot cream, massage oil, relaxing bath
- Oropax
- Energy bars, gels, sports drink
- Toilet tissue, handkerchief
- Marathon program
- Money in local currency

**In the hand luggage:**

- Shoes, socks and clothes for the marathon, race confirmation (registration card)

# QUESTIONS AND ANSWERS

## How many marathons a year?

After a marathon, about two months will pass until your body has fully recovered. That's why the best runners in the world participate in only two marathons a year and attach importance to the fact that at least five months are in-between the two races.

## How healthy is a marathon?

A marathon is an enormous stress for the whole body. The energy reserves get completely emptied, the body liquid gets out of balance, many electrolytes get lost, the immune system becomes temporary weak, muscles and joints get extremely punished. In short, running 42.195 kilometers is not very healthy, but the training you do before the marathon is.

## Can a marathon damage the heart?

Under normal circumstances, a healthy heart cannot get damaged, but a diseased one may very well be hurt. Unrecognized illnesses, even a common flu or a cardiac defect, are responsible for most of the deaths that occur now and then in city marathons. But even drugs, doping or exaggerated ambitions may eliminate the pain threshold and overtax the heart. Therefore, sports physicians all over the world recommend a check-up before you begin with the marathon training if you are over 35 years old.

## What about the food?

It is not the one who eats a lot who can increase his performance but the one who eats right. For all endurance athletes, carbohydrates are very important. They are supposed to be proportionately 60-65% of the overall nutrition. The rest consists of fat (approximately 20%) and protein (approximately 15%). Pasta, rice, potatoes and bread are ideal suppliers of carbohydrates. At the same time a sufficient liquid intake is also very important. Every person needs at least 2 liters per day. Endurance athletes are supposed to add 1 to 1 $^1/_2$ liters per hour.

## Is track training useful?

There is a feeling that the running track is only for the young and fit, for high performance athletes, but this is not the case. The good things about running tracks: You have a traffic-free all-weather surface to run on (even in winter). You know exactly how far you are running. A lap on the inside lane is 400m. This is important, for example, when you want to know your anaerobic threshold and you go for the 10km test run. (See half-marathon in Chapter 4). Running on the track gives you a chance to meet up with other runners. On the other hand, too much track running can lead to injuries. And because you know exactly how far you are running, you cannot cheat yourself about your state of fitness.

## Where does the marathon distance come from?

At the inaugural Olympic games in 1896 in Athens, the distance of the marathon was about 40 kilometers from the small town of Marathon to the Panathinaikon Stadium in Athens.

It was only twelve years later, at the London Olympics, when the marathon became its strange length of 26 miles and 385 yards (42.195km) because the royal family wanted to watch the start in front of the Windsor Castle.

For unexplained reasons, this abstruse distance was adopted as official for all Olympics, beginning with the 1924 games in Paris.

# Chapter 7

## DOCTOR ROSA'S SECRETS

Behind Paul Tergat's successes there is a coach from Italy: "Dottore" Gabriele Rosa. Now you might think, of course, an Italian physician, they have been in the headlines again and again because of doping accusations, haven't they? And some of them were even brought to court.

Indeed, Professor Francesco Conconi got famous first of all because of the test named after him for defining the anaerobic threshold, but also as a modern "Doctor Mabuse" who was working for many years together with coach Pier-Paolo Lenzi at Ferrara and who brought a lot of long distance runners, lead by Orlando Pizzolato, the two times winner of the New York marathon, and Salvatore Betiol in a miraculous way to the limelight. Even cross country skiers and cyclist Marco Pantani, who in the meantime died of an overdose, belonged to the biochemist's clients at Ferrara. It is assumed he first manipulated the athletes by using blood doping and later EPO. Conconi's disciple Dr. Michele Ferrari counted and still counts a lot of prominent professional cyclists as his clients, even six-time Tour de France winner Lance Armstrong. The Russian cyclist Pavel Tonkov once said: "There was the talk when you go there, you get faster." It was a time when many professional cyclists suddenly had increased haematocrit levels.

No prosecutor investigated Dr. Rosa, even though he, too, is an Italian doctor, and one who took many athletes to the top. Rosa has always kept his distance from people like Conconi and Ferrari and has never worked for the Italian athletics federation (FIDAL) or the national Olympic committee (CONI). From the beginning, he went his own way. A runner when he joined high school, Rosa started coaching some athletes when he was still a student. Later, he took over the coaching of some marathon runners from his home area. In 1978, more than ten years after his first attempt, he started a very successful collaboration with Gianni Poli who was a young upcoming Italian runner, and when Poli won the prestigious New York City Marathon in the year 1986, this was a breakthrough for "Dottore". Many international athletes now wanted to work with him. Subsequently, the contact with Moses Tanui, who was one of the best Kenyan runners at the time, took place. In 1992, Rosa started the project "Discovery Kenya," which, after a short time with K-Way, was sponsored by the Italian sports brand Fila (which has since been sold to an American investment group).

Gabriele Rosa is an aristocrat. He bears the name of his great-grandfather who was one of the heroes of the Risorgimento, the Italian unification movement in the 19th century. His house outside Brescia, where his son Marco is the head of the "Centro Marathon" clinic, looks like an art gallery.

*Dr. Rosa receives a goat as a sign of appreciation from Tergat's father*

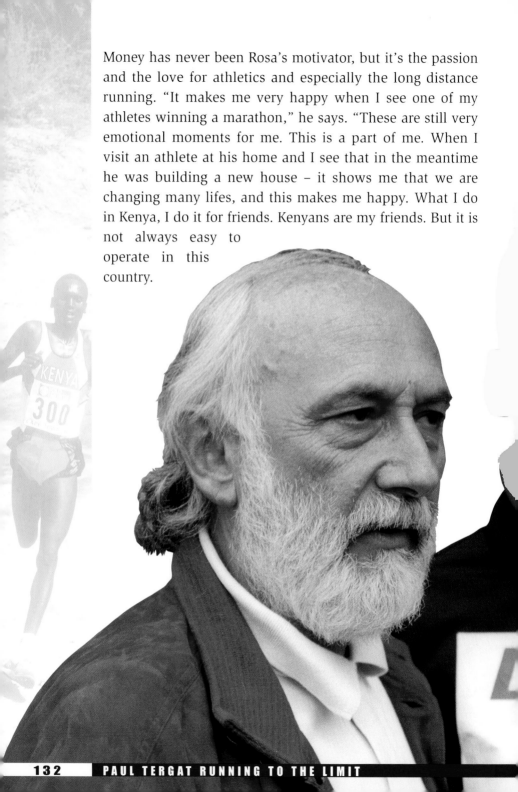

Money has never been Rosa's motivator, but it's the passion and the love for athletics and especially the long distance running. "It makes me very happy when I see one of my athletes winning a marathon," he says. "These are still very emotional moments for me. This is a part of me. When I visit an athlete at his home and I see that in the meantime he was building a new house – it shows me that we are changing many lifes, and this makes me happy. What I do in Kenya, I do it for friends. Kenyans are my friends. But it is not always easy to operate in this country.

One day the chairman of Athletics Kenya may invite me for dinner, the following day he accuses me of burning out the young athletes. Nevertheless, not only for a lot of young people in Kenya a dream came true but also for me."

"Doctor," as they call him respectfully, is the most successful marathon coach the world has ever seen. Before Gabriele Rosa started to coach runners in the East African country, the Kenyan marathon runners hardly existed. In 1990 there was only one Kenyan, Douglas Wakiihuri, among the 20 fastest runners of the year, the next two, Ibrahim Hussein and Daniel Nzioka, betwen position 80 and 100. (By the way: Wakiihuri lived in Japan, Hussein in the USA). Fourteen years later you will find that under the first 100 names, every second one is a Kenyan. And the great majority of them belong to the same "stable."

Doctor Rosa was the one who transformed Kenya into the leading country of marathon runners. Marathon didn't have a tradition here. All the athletes liked to run cross country. Even Paul Tergat preferred it. For decades, there were good Kenyan coaches when it came to cross country. For the track they were mediocre but for marathon training, they hadn't an idea. The mentality was like this for a long time: a marathoner has to run three or four hours at a slow pace. Rosa came and changed the training completely to include more quality, individuality and purpose. He was establishing a number of training camps. The first one came to life in 1993 at Kaptagat Hotel. A little later, he built his own camp at the same place where there is a forest and hilly roads.

*The training camp at Kaptagat*

After Kaptagat, many other training camps were established because the athletes who reached good results asked Doctor to open new ones at the places where they lived, thus bringing opportunities to many other young people. This is how all in all 12 training camps were born, among them ones at Kapsabet, Kapkoi, Ngong and Mount Elgon.

The latest was opened in January 2003 at Kapsait in the Cherangani Hills at 3000m above sea level with a capacity of 100 athletes. At this place where the world seems to end there is no electricity and no network for mobile phones. The athletes' lives consist of training, sleeping and eating.

*The camp at Kapsait; Rosa in traditional outfit with dignitaries at the opening ceremony*

Rosa's idea was to gather many athletes in the same camps and teach them not only a training method but also a lifestyle. "It is necessary to dedicate all day to the training program," Rosa says. This is how a day in his camps looks like:

|  |  |
|---|---|
| 6:30 a.m.: | morning training |
| 9:00 a.m.: | breakfast |
| 10:00 a.m.: | relax or personal activities |
| 12:30 p.m.: | lunch |
| 2:30 p.m.: | relax |
| 4:30 p.m.: | second training |
| 7:30 p.m.: | supper |
| 9:30 p.m.: | sleep |

This kind of timetable does not only give the course of the day but also the way of life. The athletes who join are obligated to leave their families, their friends and their jobs for months to become authentic professionals. Rosa says "My philosophy can be synthesized in a few words: training twice a day, relax and correct diet."

In Kenya, all the marathoners belonging to Rosa's company, Rosassociati, are following the same training programs, written by Doctor himself. In the last three months prior to a marathon, the program has the following features:

- the mileage is between 210 and 240 kilometers each week
- the intensity of the training rises more and more every week until the last two weeks when the work load is reduced drastically
- the weekly work load is repetitive and consists of:
  - a long run, which can change between 35 and 38km
  - a session of short repetitions on the track
  - a session of long repetitions on the track
  These so-called technical sessions alternate with a day of two trainings between 1h and 1h15', always of good quality.

(For more details, go to Chapter 5 and see Tergat's program for the 2002 London marathon.)

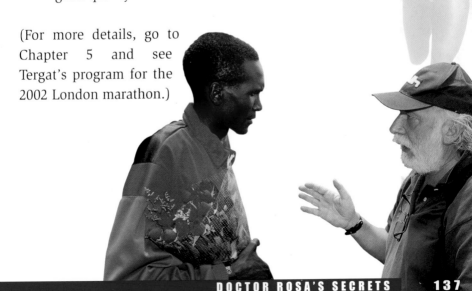

Local coaches take care that the athletes stay on course. Gabriele Rosa himself or his son Federico travel to Kenya on a regular basis to make sure everything is going well. The athletes are in shape when they are called for a race. They always go for fast long runs up to 38km. "We know how fast somebody has to cover the distance when he wants to run the marathon in 2:06 or 2:07 hours," Rosa explains.

**P.T.:** *"When Doctor Rosa started coaching me, I entered a new world. All of a sudden we did a lot of speed work and speed endurance on the track, something I had never done before. When I think about the 7:28 at 3,000m, I as a cross country and long distance runner was able to run in 1996 – this was the result of his training. When we talk about Doctor Rosa as a person, he is very friendly and professional. Indeed, sometimes he has a hot temper and in the eyes of people who don't know him well he might seem arrogant. But I know him as a very likeable and just person whose world is running. At the beginning of our relationship, he was the coach. In the course of the years, he became a very close friend of mine, as well as my family. I believe my wife is the only person who knows and understands me better than him."*

*Sports minister Balala with Rosa and other dignitaries (Sang, Hussein and Keino in the background)*

Doctor Rosa's company is by far the strongest power when it comes to marathon in Kenya. About 40 people are working for Rosassociati in Kenya, including part-time coaches.

They operate 12 different training camps. All in all, there are about 200 athletes. Most of them stay in the camps. A number of young ones, for whom the company pays the school fees, still live at home or are in boarding schools.

There is no other team with so many marathon victories and positions under the first three in the last few years:

**2000:**    22 gold, 21 silver, 19 bronze
(53 marathon participations)

**2001:**    24 gold, 21 silver, 22 bronze
(55 marathon participations)

**2002:**    39 gold, 28 silver, 27 bronze
(72 marathon participations)

**2003:**    36 gold, 27 silver, 25 bronze
(62 marathon participations)

**2004:**    27 gold, 25 silver, 23 bronze
(69 marathon participations)

**Paul Tergat:** won a record number of five world cross country titles, two in half-marathon, broke World Records at 10,000m in 1997 (26:27,85), in half-marathon 1998 (59:17) and in marathon 2003 (2:04,55 in Berlin)

**Moses Tanui:** won the world title at 10,000m in 1991 and in half-marathon 1995, Boston marathon winner 1996 and 1998, World Record in half-marathon 1993 (59:47)

**Margaret Okayo:** won marathons in San Diego 2000 and 2001, New York 2001 and 2003, Boston 2002, Milan 2002 and London 2004

**Martin Lel:** won the World Half-marathon Championship and the New York marathon 2003

**Sammy Korir:** won marathons in Florence and Cancún 1996, Amsterdam 1997 and 1999, Turin 1999, Beppu and San Diego 2002; second to Tergat in Berlin 2003

**Joseph Chebet:** won marathons in Amsterdam 1996, Turin 1997, Boston and New York 1999

**Elijah Lagat:** won marathons in Jerez 1994, Berlin 1997, Prague 1998 and Boston 2000

**Robert Cheruiyot:** won the Boston marathon 2003

**Charles Kamathi:** won the World Championship at 10,000m 2001

(Many others have won competitions all over the world.)

Rosa's team organizes different races in Kenya, especially in and around Eldoret: The Fila Discovery cross country was established already in 1993 and is, in the meantime, with more than 2,000 runners, among them even small children who just run for fun, the biggest cross country in the whole of Kenya. There is also a half-marathon and a 10km road race.

No doubt about it, these races are not only for giving local runners an opportunity, they are used also by the company's scouts for recruiting new athletic talent. For somebody who has spent many millions of dollars improving and helping the running scene in Kenya, this is actually absolutely legitimate. There are enough black sheep, so-called "managers" from Europe who just come to Kenya for milking the athletes, without investing anything in the development of the Kenyan sport.

Apart from the permanent camps, Rosa's people are also organizing periodical camps for young athletes. Here is an example of a training program the way it is used at the Kaptarakwa camp for preparing the cross country season (2 weeks):

## TRAINING PROGRAM KAPTARAKWA CAMP FOR YOUNG ATHLETES (PREPARATION FOR THE CROSS-COUNTRY SEASON)

| Day | Early Morning | Mid-Morning | Afternoon |
|---|---|---|---|
| Monday: | Hill training 200-300m medium-fast (60-80% effort) | *Striding 200m x 10 | 40-50min easy (50-60%) |
| Tuesday: | 60min long run (50%) | Speed training 200m x 10, 300m x 10 (90%) | 50min easy (50-60%) |
| Wednesday: | 50min easy (50-60%) | Diagonals, 50 min | – |
| Thursday: | 40min fast pace (80-90%) | (Class teaching on training) | 40min easy (50-60%) |
| Friday: | 40-50min easy- medium (50-70%) | Exercises | 40min jogging (50%) |
| Saturday: | 70min long run (50%) | (Cleaning) | (Cleaning) |
| Sunday: | 60min easy-medium (50-70%) | – | – |
| Monday: | 50min easy (50-60%) | 35min medium (70%) | 60min fartlek |
| Tuesday: | 50min medium (70%) | Exercises | Striding 300m x 15 |
| Wednesday: | 60min long run (50%) | – | 35-40min diagonals |
| Thursday: | 40min easy (50-60%) | 30min easy (50-60%) | 12km fast pace (90%) |
| Friday: | 60min long run (50%) | Striding, 30min | 50min easy (50-60%) |
| Saturday: | Camp competitions | – | 40-50min easy (50-60%) |

*Remarks: The main objectives are aerobic training and speed endurance.*
   *\* Striding means technical runs*

# ROSA'S TIPS FOR SERIOUS RUNNERS

It is pointless for somebody to go for a three-week training at high altitude only once a year. High-altitude training makes only sense if you stay there for a longer period or several times a year for some weeks.

On the other hand, there is no doubt that endurance athletes, such as long distance runners, can benefit from the high altitude where you increase the red blood cells that are vital for oxygen transport. Robert de Castella, Steve Jones, Arturo Barrios, Uta Pippig and other world-class athletes all decided to stay in Boulder, Colorado at an altitude equivalent with the Kenyan highlands. The body adapts after some time to the new conditions, meaning it has more hemoglobin at its disposal and therefore a better oxygen intake.

According to our studies, even a stay at about 4,000m above sea level for 10 or 12 days will lead to a significant hemoglobin increase (for example, around the lake of Titicaca on the border area between Bolivia and Peru). However, somebody who decides to train at such an extreme height has to follow some rules: You have to be already in a very good shape when you go there because you can only jog, let's say two times one hour of easy running a day. Three weeks before your competition, you should return to the lowlands where you can do a few more quality workouts.

I am convinced that training in a hilly area is very important for marathon runners. Somebody who always runs on the flat will after some time lose his strength. The other point is the mileage. Indeed, Paul Tergat has weeks when he covers almost 300 kilometers, but he is an exception. For me, the quality is always much more important than the quantity. I think even top marathoners don't need to run more than 240 kilometers a week. At the same time, I don't believe in a one-hour run at a 4-minute pace, either. My top athletes start maybe at 4'20'' per kilometer and end the session at 3'20'' or 3'10''. I am a strong supporter of so-called progressive running.

Probably the most important advice for a long distance runner who wants to move up to the marathon: Be patient. It takes years to transform a 10,000m runner into a good marathoner. Don't forget: When you run the 10,000m, your body is consuming a lot of four-star petrol. In the marathon, a different biochemistry takes place.

You have to use your glycogen economically and burn fat, too. Your body will learn how to burn fat only after a lot of long runs.

Apart from this fact, even the running technique is different compared with running on the track where you land much more on the forefoot. It took Moses Tanui three years to adapt even though he was already a successful runner at the half-marathon distance. In the meantime, he has won Boston two times and, with a personal best of 2:06:16, he still is one of the fastest marathon runners of all time.

You should also be aware that not every good long distance runner will become a good marathoner. Me, I personally believe that Haile Gebrselassie, the undisputed long distance king of the nineties, is not meant for the marathon. Of course he ran 2:06:35 in his first marathon 2002 in London, but to me this is not the proof yet.

We have seen in cross country that he is not a champion on all surfaces. He was very strong on the track and especially indoors where the track is somewhat springy. This suits his jumping style. On the road, one has to run more economically if he doesn't want to risk injury. We have to wait and see if he can adjust to these new requirements.

**Dr. Gabriele Rosa's suggestions for serious hobby athletes:**

*"Train yourself to enjoy yourself and to improve your physical shape"*

*Two distinguished couples: the Rosas and the Tergats at the IAAF gala in Monaco*

# Chapter 8

## CROWNING IN BERLIN

His wife, Monica, was waiting for him at the finish line. And when he arrived after an incredible 2 hours, 4 minutes and 55 seconds, she was the first person to congratulate him. She hugged him for a very long time, tears in her eyes. Monica Tergat knew how much her husband sacrificed for this moment and she alone could tell how much he longed for this World Record. He had punished himself to the limit.

**P.T.:** *"My wife was the only person who knew almost one year ago already that I am going to try a World Record. She was the only person who was supporting me in the hard times of the training. She was the only one*

*I wanted to watch me competing and be close to me. And we shared this moment. It was very sweet for us, especially for her after seeing what I have gone through: all the tough training, the sacrifices, sometimes sleeping very early and getting up very early, not being able to see the children going to school. It was a huge effort. People don't know what lies behind such an achievement. The joy and the emotions when you win a big race or break a record, this is what compensates you for all the hard training. Even after finishing three times second and two times fourth I still carried the belief inside me. I never believe something is impossible before I try."*

Tergat had been very disappointed with his race in London back in April 2003 when he was almost forced to drop out because of stomach problems and was eventually relegated to the fourth position in the final sprint. That's why he started the preparation for Berlin as early as May when he called his two pacemakers Titus Munji and Michael Rotich and some other runners to his Ngong home where they trained together for more than three months. Of course Chicago wanted him back, but Tergat gave Berlin precedence even if he didn't receive the same appearance money. The Berlin organizers with father, Horst and son, Mark Milde had promised to assist him as much as they could so that his dream could come true. The problem in many of his previous marathons was that when there are too many strong athletes in the field, the race always becomes tactical. People forget about running fast, what matters is only the victory.

Before Berlin, he changed the training slightly: more long runs but more moderate, because in the previous marathons he always had problems on the last one or two kilometers. He had realized that in a marathon a lot depends on the mental ability after 38km. This is why he increased his longest training runs from 38 to 40km and once he covered 45 kilometers in 2:29 on a difficult course with a tough hill. He ran these 45km so that in the marathon, the 42 seem to be somehow short. Tergat decided to do this immensely long run on his own. It was only after the race that he dared to tell coach Rosa about it. The mileage increased up to almost 300 kilometers a week. Too much? "It worked out incredibly."

**P.T.:** *"I didn't go for the money. I wanted to break the World Record. I didn't have any other business. I was not hiding, I announced it a long time ago. And knowing that I will go for the record gave me a huge motivation. And then this 28th September arrived. It was the perfect race, the weather and the flat course were ideal. I didn't have any problems on the way, but without the help of my friends it would not have been possible. God gave me very strong guys who were in the best form and who were willing to assist me. You cannot break a marathon World Record if you have to run alone for the last seven or even ten kilometers. I give a lot of credit to the pacemakers, especially Titus Munji and Sammy Korir who did an amazing job."*

Korir lives and trains in Eldoret with the group of Fred Kiprop and has been running marathons for seven years, never breaking the 2:08 barrier. He was supposed to run the Amsterdam marathon but was informed only one week before the Berlin race that he was to be Tergat's pacemaker. During the race, he decided he was going all the way to the finish line. Korir crossed the line only one second behind Tergat in 2:04:56. It was the first time in 15 years that two runners broke the World Record in the same marathon. Tergat became just the second man, besides legendary Finn Johannes Kohlemainen, to have set a 10,000 meters World Record and run the fastest marathon time in history.

Did Tergat ever fear he could lose the race and the record to Korir – who turned out to be a real sensation? "Not for one minute," he says. "I was very strong. I was always in control of the race, even if he had tricked me. After 35km I knew he was a competitor, around 40 he was a rival, a potential winner. That's why I made the move around 41. Unfortunately I lost most of my lead at the Brandenburg Gate when I was confused and didn't know where to pass." Berlin was using a new route that year and the city officials refused to let the guiding blue line be painted on the part of the street that went trough the gate.

Was the 2:04:55 the best result possible? Tergat thinks it over before saying: "On this day, it was the best possible, but I believe there is a good chance to run 2:04:30 soon. Under 2:04 will be for the next generation." When asked what was the hardest part of the race, his answer was surprising.

**P.T.:** *"The hours after the race were the hardest. You feel tired, your body is aching, but you have to go from one interview to the other, you have to smile to I don't know how many cameras. Everybody wants something from you."*

## TERGAT VS. KHANNOUCHI

Paul Tergat's pace was behind that of previous marathon World Record setter, Khalid Khannouchi, throughout almost the entire race.

| | Khannouchi, London 2002, 2:05:38 | | Tergat, Berlin 2003, 2:04:55 | |
|------|---------|---------|---------|---------|
| 5km | 14:44 | | 15:00 | |
| 10km | 29:37 | (14:53) | 29:55 | (14:55) |
| 15km | 44:35 | (14:58) | 44:45 | (14:50) |
| 20km | 59:33 | (14:58) | 59:43 | (14:58) |
| 25km | 1:14:10 | (14:37) | 1:14:42 | (14:59) |
| 30km | 1:29:01 | (14:51) | 1:29:24 | (14:42) |
| 35km | 1:43:58 | (14:57) | 1:43:59 | (14:35) |
| 40km | 1:59:11 | (15:13) | 1:58:36 | (14:37) |
| | | | | |
| Half | 1:02:47 | | 1:03:01 | |

When he arrived back at the hotel four hours after finishing the 42.195m, Tergat was exhausted. He was able to relax a little before he went for dinner with Monica, Korir, Munji, Rotich, coach Gabriele Rosa and his son Federico. But before 11 they had to be back at the official reception and awards ceremony with the organizers. No wonder Tergat did not find any sleep after such a demanding day. But he was far from complaining: "When you are happy, you don't care." Three weeks later Tergat was still feeling pain in his legs while running downhill.

*The new number plate: 204 B for 2:04 Berlin*

Kenya's newspapers had almost ignored Tergat's trip to Berlin. This only caused greater surprise and joy when the news of the World Record spread. And when the new national hero arrived at the Jomo Kenyatta airport that Wednesday morning, there were hundreds of people waiting for him. Relatives and neighbors from his home area in the Baringo District traveled in buses all night long to reach Nairobi on time.

*Paul Tergat at the reception in Nairobi with the insignias of a warrior*

It was the biggest welcome for a Kenyan athlete since independence 40 years ago. Sports minister Balala was the head of the congratulators in the overcrowded VIP room. He promised that "very soon" an important road in Nairobi would be named after Tergat. Politicians gathered around him to be in photos. Outside the airport, traditional dancers were waiting for their hero and provided him with the insignias of a successful warrior. From the hands of his mother he received a gourd filled with "mursiik," the traditional sour milk.

In the afternoon, the celebrations continued "en famille" at Tergat's Ngong home. The following day, Tergat had yet another very busy schedule. He woke up at 6 to take a flight to Eldoret, the "capital city of running," where people, such as Kipchoge Keino, Ibrahim Hussein, Moses Tanui, Patrick Sang, Yobes Ondieki, Moses Kiptanui, Noah Ngeny, Daniel Komen, Bernard Barmasai, Reuben Kosgei, Japhet Kimutai, Sammy Korir and Stephen Cherono (Said Saeef Shaheen), lived. The convoy was welcomed at a reception at the Town Hall and Tergat was asked to sign the visitors' book. They proceeded along cleared roads with at least 40 escorting cars to the birthplace of Sammy Korir. Tergat received the traditional gifts: a gourd in the one hand and two or three blankets around his neck.

*Titus Munji, Paul Tergat and Sammy Korir*

*At the home of Sammy Korir, below: Korir, Tergat and Munji*

After these tiring two days, the marathon hero conceded himself one week off before he started the final lap of honor which consisted of a triumphant procession in an open Land Cruiser from his second home at Kabarak near Nakuru to Riwo. The celebrations were held at the "Riwo Primary School" where Paul Tergat went to school 20 years ago.

*The celebrations at Riwo.*
*Below: the Tergat and the Wirz couple, on the left: Tergat's mother*

Groups of women and pupils were singing and dancing, there were many speeches (Kenyans like making speeches), but the highlight of the ceremony was still to come. Tergat was fitted with an animal skin and promoted to a "Tugen elder," meaning that whenever there is a problem in the Tugen community – like the Nandi, they belong to the Kalenjin – the marathon king will be consulted. Besides him, the Tugen have only two other elders: Daniel arap Moi, the former president of the country, and his son Gideon Moi.

Usually for one to be able to be given this title, which is for life, it has to be a very exceptional performance. It can even go for decades or centuries before they announce another elder. Tergat received the greatest honor a Tugen can get not only because of his enormous success in sports but also because of his achievements in the Riwo community and because he never forgot his roots. When he is back in Riwo, he can still go to the local shop and have a tea with the village people. There he tries to explain to them that in life nothing is impossible.

At the end of all the celebrations Tergat was tired but happy. He was also proud to be the first Kenyan to have broken the World Record in marathon.

**P.T.:** *"The receptions and the celebrations were very emotional. I realized that the Kenyans see me now in a different light. This record has a lot of significance to me. It summarizes my whole career. It is the apex of my life as an athlete. All that I have done before has come together. This is definitely a new dimension, my greatest achievement ever. I have competed on the track, in cross country and on the road. Now I can proudly say: This is the mother of running. Whether you are jogging or running on the top level – the marathon is the dream of all of us. Whether you try to break the 4 hours barrier or the World Record we have to fight to succeed. And I believe it is the toughest of all the World Records. In a marathon, you enter no man's land after 38 kilometers. The body starts paining, the legs want to stop, only your mind keeps you going."*

## TERGAT'S THOUGHTS

- If you want to achieve something special, a personal best, a record or breaking a barrier, you have to sacrifice yourself. In training, there is no shortcut.

- Never think something is impossible before you try. When you say it is impossible, that means you have given up already.

- Never blame your personal surroundings when you are not able to reach your goals. It is not your background that counts but what you make out of your life. Your destiny lies in your hands.

*They were engaged "forever" before they married in November 1994*

# Chapter 9

# THE FAMILY AND BUSINESS MAN

Paul Tergat is soft spoken, but he is also well spoken. His press conferences are well attended because, whether in victory or defeat, he is ever jovial, a true gentleman and a true sportsman. He is liked by competitors as well as big business people and politicians around the world, but also by millions of fans. He managed to remain simple and ordinary in a glittering world of sports celebrities.

**P.T.:** *"It is a good feeling when you go around and everybody knows you. They are identifying you with something good. I feel very honored. People appreciate what I have done for Kenyan sports – and especially that I brought the World Record in marathon to this* *country. It is amazing how many people admire my performances. On the other hand, so many want to be part of my success, so many want something. It makes life a bit difficult but also sweet if you know how to balance your schedule. And frankly I have quite a lot of people working for me for all my different business activities. They are blocking out all the unimportant requests and wishes. My job is running. As long as I am a professional runner, I have to focus fully on my training. And apart from my running, I need to have also time for my family. I have an obligation to be near my growing children. I would hate if they would ask me one day why I was never there for them."*

## THE FAMILY MAN

He says his wife Monica ("She is the dearest wife in the world") is the one who made him who he is. He admits that if she would not have been very strong in taking care of the family, he could not have achieved anything. When the children were still very young, he was travelling all over the world. She always gave him a lot of encouragement, even though she had never been an athlete herself and didn't know a lot about running. Monica Tergat is a nurse at a government hospital, and if everything goes well, she will get her degree in 2005. What an amazing story itself.

Paul and Monica are from the same Riwo area. They knew and liked each other when they were very young. Paul calls it "a natural love." They were engaged "forever" before they married in November 1994. Monica knew and accepted his humble background. She loved him for who he was and not for what he had, because even when they married, he didn't have a lot. Neither ever forgot where they came from.

And even now that they have the money to send their three children, Ronald, Harriet and Gloria to very good schools, they want them to know that in life there are more important things than money.

*Holidays in Zanzibar*

For Paul, the family is the source of his mental strength. On the other hand, when a member of the family has a problem or is sick, it disturbs him a lot. The hard fighting athlete is a very sensitive husband and father.

# THE BUSINESS MAN

Even if he has made millions of dollars through running, Tergat has never been the kind of athlete who likes or needs to show off with a lot of brand new cars or a new super villa. His wife Monica drives a second hand car, and the house he lives in with his family was built in 1997. It is on the top of a hill at Ngong outside Nairobi next to Karen, made famous in the book and subsequent film – *Out of Africa*. For an athlete of his caliber, the house is quite modest.

It should not be kept a secret that, in the course of the years, he purchased a big farm of 40 acres at Turbo in the Northwest of the country and, at Kabarak near Nakuru, he has a second home in the direct neighborhood of Daniel Arap Moi, the former president of Kenya, with 80 acres of farm land. There he has also put up a house for his mother who is a very cheerful, strong person, full of life.

*The new house at Kabarak in the neighborhood of former President Moi*

All in all, he has almost 100 cows for milking. It seems in the future Kabarak will be the home of Paul and Monica Tergat.

Paul Tergat doesn't like to talk about money, or his investments. But at the same time, he is very much aware that in a book on his life this is something people wish to know about. One thing is for sure: Tergat was investing his money wisely from the beginning of his career, knowing that it could be over any day. After the injury he sustained in 1992 he knew, as an athlete, there is no guarantee. He is conscious of Mike Tyson's situation, a man who earned millions of dollars as a boxer but has lost most of it. Tergat has his money in different banks and companies.

*The inner courtyard of the Sportsline Hotel at Karbarnet when it was still under construction*

Tergat bought and built some houses at Ngong and in Nairobi, a hotel in his home district Kabarnet, he is the owner and publisher of *The Athlete*, the only magazine in East Africa specializing in track and field events. He has a lot of different shares, most of them in Kenya but also in Italy, the country where he used to stay very often when he was still a track runner. One of his brothers is taking care of the farm at Turbo, and for the other businesses he has an office in Nairobi with ten people working for him. His guess is that almost 100 people work for him. This alone shows how big his empire is. But when it comes to the stock exchange he likes pulling the strings himself.

## THE MILITARY MAN

After 1992, Tergat was exempt from the daily duties of his Air Force unit, but he still has to go there from time to time and has had to represent the Armed Forces when it comes to National Championships, either on the track or in cross country. These days he has special tasks concerning sports. He now has the rank of a Warrant Officer Two.

A few days after his World Record in Berlin, Tergat was on the way to the Moi Air Base. The choking smoke spewed by speeding matatus (mini busses for the public transport) makes driving fast a nuisance, and dangerous. Misery and poverty can be felt along the road that neighbors the Mathare slum. A man in a green Mercedes Benz is sandwiched between two noisy matatus. But he is calm as he nonchalantly watches life around him.

*Warrant Officer Tergat (with the silver star of the Republic of Kenya) together with running colleague Captain Paul Koech and a friend*

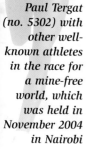

These scenes always remind him on his roots – poverty. He has used this route many times. Slowly, he drives down the road up to the Moi Air Base turnoff where the gate is opened with haste. Although in civilian attire – a black designer suit, blue shirt and matching tie – Senior Sergeant Paul Tergat has finally reported to work. But today he has come to debrief his superiors on what he has been doing since his time out a month ago. He will tell them about the days in Berlin.

## THE PHILANTHROPIST

Throughout most of his adult life, Paul Tergat has handled a lot of responsibilities, but not only for his extended family. He has given a lot of support and initiates projects in his home area of Riwo. He helped to establish health facilities and bring clean water and electricity to the center. He has been trying to help children go through school and support themselves. He has sought scholarships for those who excel in school in the United Kingdom and the United States. And he is on the way to establishing a foundation that will help young people to get a good education.

*Paul Tergat (no. 5302) with other well-known athletes in the race for a mine-free world, which was held in November 2004 in Nairobi*

Tergat believes there are only a few who are left out of school because of having a learning disability but many bright children who don't have the opportunity to attend a good school. The foundation would also help to buy the books and stationery children who cannot afford it. Another goal would be establishing health centers in the rural areas where even today many people still die because they have no health care. And finally, exchange programs and scholarships for young athletes would be organized.

On May 27, 2003, Paul Tergat received an honorary bachelor of arts in physical education and public service from Bloomfield College in the United States for his involvement in charitable and philanthropic activities. "Paul Tergat has not only proved to be an outstanding athlete in competitions across the globe, but already, at 34, is a philanthropist in his own right, an exemplary global citizen," said professor Sandy Van Dyk, who nominated him for the honorary degree. The Community Baptist Church of Eaglewood, New Jersey, proclaimed November 1, 2003, "Paul Tergat Day" in his honor, celebrating his achievements in sports, his courage and humanity.

*Tergat with members of the Community Baptist Church of Eaglewood*

# THE UN AMBASSADOR AGAINST HUNGER

At the end of 2003, Paul Tergat was appointed as a UN World Food Program Goodwill Ambassador. When Tergat grew up in a humble environment in the Baringo District, he was one of hundreds of children who profited from the WFP's free daily school-lunch program for quite some time. In Kenya, the school-lunch program, also supported by the government, is one of the most extensive and longstanding programs, dating back to the 1980s. Over a million school children have benefited from it.

*A big moment: Appointment as a UN Goodwill ambassador against Hunger, with WFP director James Morris*

**P.T.:** *"I feel honored to be a part of this program. There is a lot of hunger in this world and a lot of children are dropping out of school. It saddens me that in the 21st century we still have a very big problem of hunger in this world. I feel I have an obligation to give something back.*

*My main role is raising awareness and funds for the school lunch program to ensure that it is sustained for a long time. I think my contacts and image around the world would have a big impact in supporting this program. I believe strongly that without education there is no progress in any country. Illiteracy should be kicked out of this world completely. The future of this world is in these children we are trying to keep in school."*

In his role as an ambassador for the World Food Program, Tergat travels not only within Kenya but also to different African countries, including Sudan and Somalia.

# THE ATHLETICS PROMOTER

In 2003, Tergat and his office also started to organize some races for young athletes in Kenya. But his approach is very different from others who have only one target: They want to recruit talents and sign them up for their management companies. Tergat looked for a national company that wanted to give something back to the community and support the idea as a sponsor. He found that company in Tarda, a big nationally operating corporation that produces different food stuffs and dairy products. Tergat says they don't necessarily want to recruit athletes and send them abroad. They don't want the agents necessarily to benefit from the project. The most important thing is to bring a running awareness to the localities. In the rural areas of the country, especially in the eastern part, is where they organize most of the races. This area is very poor, very dry. There were very few athletes coming from this part of the country. Cosmas Ndeti and Patrick Ivuti were two of them. According to Tergat, the support and the attendance at these competitions is very high.

**P.T.:** *"I am happy to see that a lot of strong athletes were already coming out of our project. The main idea behind it is that any athlete who is performing well and has already finished school gets a job from the sponsor company. Tarda gives them an opportunity to earn a living, so that they can progress in their sports career. Secondly, for the ones who are still in high school, the company pays the school fees."*

## MEMBER OF THE IAAF ATHLETE'S COMMISSION

Since 2003, Tergat is also a member of the IAAF athlete's commission. He is proud of this role, especially because the voting was done at the World Championships in Paris where he was not even present.

*Together with David Okeyo, general secretary of Athletics Kenya*

Like all the others on the comitee, he was elected for a four-year term. He intends not only to be at the meetings and bring his ideas and opinions but he also will identify the concerns of other active athletes around the world. In this context Tergat calls the IAAF World Ranking, introduced in 2001, as very strange, because a marathon runner who can only run two races a year is practically excluded. (In 2004, the IAAF started a ranking for roadrunners. They have to score in three events, but the track athletes must score in six.)

**P.T.:** *"When it comes to the athlete of the year award, a marathon runner has no chance to win because he has only two races that count," he says. "For a long time the road racers were only second-class athletes. Now at least the records are recognized as official World Records and not only best times."*

*Even the White House acknowledges Tergat's merits*

*Paul Tergat with Tegla Loroupe at an IAAF gala*

*In the middle of beauty queens he feels at home, too*

# PAUL TERGAT IN THE FUTURE

Even after retiring from running, Tergat will never lean back and enjoy the "dolce far niente," even if he admits that he will take life easier after all the years of hard work. He is the kind of guy who always has to be busy in one way or another. He is looking forward to the time when he can get more involved personally in his businesses and when he will have time for new projects. "There are still some things I want to do after retiring as an athlete," he says. One thing is for sure: Tergat will always be in athletics. He wants to play a more active role in the national athletics scene. But he stresses that the only job he would like to do in Athletics Kenya would be the one of chairman, a position Isaiah Kiplagat holds until 2008. Tergat will not disappear from the public eye or the sport he loves so much. And he will still go on as a fun runner. "Religiously," is how he calls it. "I need to run. Running is in my blood. I am born to run."

# Chapter 10

## MISCELLANEOUS

### FEEL YOUR BODY

Kenyan athletes have the big advantage over the "wazungu" – that is what they call the white people – because they know and feel their bodies much better. It is inside them and it certainly has to do with how they live and grow up in a much more natural environment. When you walk a lot in all kind of weather conditions and when you stay in huts where the wind and sometimes even rain enters, you not only get toughened, you will also get to know your body and have a feel for it.

**P.T.:** *" I feel when my body is okay. On the other hand, when I don't feel well, I don't force myself. What matters is that at the end of a training period all the required trainings have do be done. You have to be flexible and should never do a hard training in case you are not okay. I never ran with a heart rate monitor because I don't need it. But even with my good feeling for my body and my long experience as a runner I cannot say from the way I feel if I covered the kilometer in 2:40 or 2:45. Therefore, I check the speed in the workouts where it matters on a measured route with a stopwatch.*

*Even if you don't have this sense for your body, you should never become a slave of your heart rate monitor. If you don't have a problem with your health, meaning you are not allowed to exceed a certain heart rate, leave your monitor at home more often and try to run by listening inside you. It gives you greater joy when you run in harmony with nature."*

*Women are preparing Ugali, the main Kenyan food*

# WHAT KENYANS EAT AND DRINK

Most of the Kenyan athletes come from poor families. In other words, for almost their first 20 years of life their food is very simple but healthy. The menu changes only when they join a national camp where they eat meat two times a day and when they stay in Europe or America and come into contact with French fries and hamburgers.

## This is the basic food in Kenya:

**Ugali:** A thick mash made out of boiled (white) corn/maize meal and water. At least once a day on the table.

**Sukuma Wiki:** A dark green vegetable, similar to spinach. Often served with ugali.

**Uji:** Millet or corn/maize porridge, often fermented.

**Maziwa and maziwa lala:** Normal and fermented milk.

**Viazi:** Potatoes, ordinary ones or sweet potatoes.

**Chapati:** Like an omelet but made only with flour and water.

**Maharagwe:** Beans.

**Githeri:** Corn/maize mixed and boiled with beans.

**Muthokoi:** Similar to githeri but with potatoes and pumpkin leaves.

**Matunda:** Fruits, especially green oranges, bananas, mangos and papaya.

**Chai:** "National drink" tea. The tea leaves are boiled together with half water and half milk, as well as sugar.

Carbohydrates (ugali, chapati), iron and minerals (sukuma wiki and other vegetables), protein (maziwa, maziwa lala and maharagwe) and vitamins (matunda) are part of these foods. The fat content is very low. When they boil the milk, they usually remove the fat from the surface and later use it for cooking. Meat doesn't play a role in the traditional Kenyan kitchen. Meat gets served only once every one or two weeks and often only when visitors arrive. Sugar is only found in the tea.

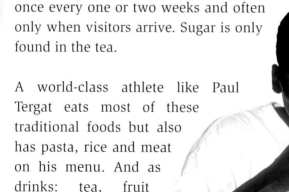

A world-class athlete like Paul Tergat eats most of these traditional foods but also has pasta, rice and meat on his menu. And as drinks: tea, fruit juices, water and from time to time a soda.

# REASONS FOR THE KENYAN SUPERIORITY

Admittedly, the Kenyan athletes didn't do very well at the Olympics in Athens. Winning only one gold medal in the steeplechase 2004 (and probably only because Said Saif Shaheen, the former Stephen Cherono, was not allowed to participate for his new country Qatar) was a disappointing outcome. Nevertheless, Kenya is still by far the dominating country in long distance running when you check the world list. In 2004, there are 37 out of 100 at 5000m, 40 at 10,000m, even 72 in the half-marathon and 48 in the marathon.

Many articles have been written, many studies have been done. Yet, there is not just one answer to the question as to why Kenyans are such good athletes. "When you are poor, you will stay poor unless you run," says the former steeplechase World Record holder and triple World Champion Moses Kiptanui. And he adds that more than 90% of the Kenyan runners who achieve international results are born poor. Motivation is a key factor. Another one is the talent. In the past, there were only few runners coming from the ethnic group of the Turkanas (Paul Ereng, Olympic

Champion at 800m in 1988) or Kikuyus (Julius Kariuki, Olympic Champion at 3,000m steeplechase in 1988). Most of the great Kenyan runners are Kalenjin (Nandi, Kipsigis, Keiyo, Marakwet, Tugen, West Pokot).

The healthy diet plays a role, too, as does the high altitude and the fact that most of the children spend their childhood walking and running barefoot. But apart from all these aspects there is one main reason: Kenyans train very, very hard. From 1992 to 1998, Tergat was running three times a day, except on Sundays. And he was not an exeption.

In the course of the years, experts from all over the world have come to Kenya to find their secret. A group of Danish scientists came to some interesting conclusions. The mass of Kenyan's lower legs were 12% less than that of Danish boys. According to the study, this explains why the running economy was found to be 10% better in the Kenyans. Apart from this fact, the Kenyans had relatively longer legs (5%). Henrik Larsen from the Copenhagen Muscle Research Centre, one of the scientists involved in the study, arrived at the following conclusion: "The low body mass and the slender legs of the Kalenjins are probably a result of the nomadic life these people were used to for generations at high altitude. To be able to move over great distances with low energy expenditure has been essential in order to survive."

## TERGAT ON DOPING, SUPPLEMENTS AND PERFORMANCE TESTS

Paul Tergat cannot recall how many times he was tested for doping in the course of his career, before and after championships or international races, as well as in out-of-competition controls. Sometimes the controllers arrive at his home as early as 6 in the morning. But he doesn't mind. He believes these tests are very important to keep the sport as clean as possible. That's why he was also a great supporter of the blood tests when they were established in the big city marathons.

**P.T.:** *"When we compete, we deserve to compete with equal opportunities. Fairness is the most important thing in sports, and this includes also fighting with spears of the same length. On the other hand, when you see the number of people who are cheating in athletics, especially in running there are very few. I am suggesting that anyone who has tested positive should be banned for life. According to me, two years is not enough. I would prefer if the IAAF would not only publish the names of the ones who were caught but also the ones who were tested with a negative result. I never took any food supplements in my life, not even vitamins. But I am not a doctor. Maybe the food in Europe and in the USA is not as balanced and fresh as what we eat in Kenya* and therefore athletes in those countries have to add these supplements. I usually go for an annual general check-up to find out if there is any substance in my body missing or under the required level. But I never had a problem. It seems we are very lucky with our food in this part of the world.

Many people believe in science. I know lactate tests are very popular even among hobby joggers. Me, I did it only once but I didn't like when they had to take my blood from the ear. I think these things are more for people who don't believe in themselves, people who need a machine to tell them."

## PLANNING IS EVERYTHING

**P.T.:** "It is really very, very important for any runner to have a long term planning. You have to know maybe half a year in advance when you are going to run your first half-marathon or marathon. It is important to have a target in your daily training. It is easier to follow a certain training program when you know exactly what you are training for.

Me I am a very busy person with all my commitments, and I could never follow my program if I would not plan properly. For my marathon training, I need two times three intensive months a year. This means all the other commitments, the business talks and activities, as well as my charity work I try to plan for the months when I have only a light training. For example, the month after the Athens Olympics, I didn't train at all but I was spending a lot of time with my family and businesses.

*You have your job, your family and your training. That means you need to include your training in your daily schedule. And when we talk about the training, I would advise everybody who wants to compete in races to follow a good program. It is easier to keep on going when you have a training program.*

*Of course if you just want to keep fit and enjoy your running, it doesn't really matter what your training looks like. But if you want to reach a target, maybe running the marathon below four hours or even three, you cannot do it without following a strict program. The best program is useless if it's only in the drawer. Admittedly, all of us have days when we would prefer staying at home. Maybe the weather is ugly or we just feel very tired after a long, stressful day. This is when discipline matters. You are allowed to change days but at the end of a period, you have to have covered all the trainings. The good thing with running is it helps you relax your mind. After coming back from a 40-minute workout you will feel much better and satisfied. And the bad mood is gone. If you have a chance of doing the training together with others, take it. It will definitely help you a lot! And by the way, keeping a diary is*

*also something that helps you to remain consistent with your training.*

*I believe that even for the one who wants to break the four hours barrier in the marathon the mental preparation is essential. Marathon is very challenging for everyone. Irrespective of what kind of a character you are, in marathon you have to be patient. At the same time, you have to be prepared for what might happen on the way, you have to be prepared for the physical pain. You have to be ready physically and mentally when you stand at the starting line and you have to focus fully on the 42.195 kilometers to come."*

## TERGAT'S ADVICE FOR YOUNG ATHLETES

**P.T.:** *"Don't compare yourself with the top athletes. Look at their achievements as future goals. You have to climb the stairs step by step. It will take years to get to your personal limit. And you have to ask yourself honestly what you believe you can achieve in your career. The goals have to be realistic. Not everybody has the talent to become a World Champion. Maybe you can break a certain barrier or become a champion on the local or national level. You will get a lot of frustrations if your goals are too high and you cannot achieve them. So many athletes give up the sport only because they didn't achieve their personal goals. But the personal goals were too high. In Kenya, I have seen so many young athletes they say they want to be like Moses Kiptanui or Daniel Komen. They try for one or two years. In the third year, they start drinking because their world has crashed and they don't see a meaning again.*

*Every year, a young athlete has to have a target. If it was a realistic one but he still didn't reach it, he has to go back to the drawing board. Together with his coach they have to analyze the situation and find the reason. Maybe the training was not right, maybe he ran too many races, maybe he had an injury or a health problem."*

## TIPS FOR SENIOR AND FUN RUNNERS

The Portuguese runner Carlos Lopes, born on February 18, 1947, achieved his best performances when he was over 37. He won the Olympic marathon 1984 in Los Angeles and in the following year, being 38 years and 34 days old, he became World Cross country Champion for the second time in a row. He crowned his career on April 20, 1985 when he broke the World Record in marathon. Lopes was 38 years and 61 days old when he ran 2:07:12 in Rotterdam, bettering Steve Jones 2:08:05 from the previous year in Chicago.

Carlos Lopes was an exception, no doubt about it. The rule is different: After 35, most good runners show a decline of about 1.5 seconds per kilometer and year.

**P.T.:** *"In case you started late with your running, there is good news for you: whatever your age, it takes about five years from getting started to reaching lifetime bests. By far the biggest improvement is made in the first couple of years. If you get the training right, performances for the late starter can go on improving into your late 40s.*

*Especially in Europe and the USA, there are lots of very good senior runners. Many are competing at the World Veteran Championships. Others start running when they are 40 or older and manage to complete their first marathon after a few years. I respect both categories of runners very much. They really impress me a lot. In Kenya, most people believe that running is only for young athletes as a way of earning one's living. They don't have the belief or understanding that running is also a very good way to keep fit. Being fat and driving a Mercedes is still a status symbol in my country. But it will change slowly but surely. Just recently I founded the Nairobi Runners Club with William Tanui and Martin Keino, son of legendary Kipchoge Keino. Our aim is to create a fun running culture and an outlet for organized running for fitness in the city. We want people to come and get professional tips on how to maintain a healthy lifestyle through running. So when you are in Nairobi you are most welcome every Saturday at 9 a.m. at the Ngong Racecourse!"*

# TRIBUTES TO TERGAT

## Haile Gebrselassie (ETH)

Tergat's longtime rival on the track, two-time Olympic Champion and four-time World Champion at 10,000m:

> *"When Paul broke the World Record in marathon, a colleague was calling me: Did you hear already? I asked him – what? I didn't know what he was talking about. Then he told me Paul Tergat broke the World Record in Berlin and ran 2:04:55. I was very excited because it was Tergat. I was so happy for him. We have been fighting a duel so many times in the past. And especially at the Olympics in Sydney when there were only nine hundreths of a second between him and me after 10,000m, I really felt for him. It was so hard for him. They should have given two gold medals. He is a wonderful athlete and a wonderful man. I respect him very much for all his achievements in cross country, on the track and on the road. And he is a real friend of mine."*

# Gabriele Rosa (ITA)

He has been Tergat's coach since 1992 and "the man behind all the successes":

*"Early 1992, a dream came true watching an athlete running in such a technical perfection on Kenyan soil. Our collaboration had a great importance for me as a coach and as a man. During the 13 years we worked together, I could experiment on more and more innovative training techniques thanks to his seriousness and availability. I think Paul Tergat is the most complete athlete who has ever existed, if we give the same dignity to cross country, road races and track. If the dream for the coach came true in meeting Paul, the dream of the man came true in knowing him as a human being. Paul is a modern, charismatic man with international views and a great communicator. He is a generous man, at hand with everybody. I believe these are the qualities which will take him at the end of his athletics career to be involved in the world of sports and then even in the political world of Kenya. The great respect we have for each other is the base of our friendship, which, I am sure, will last for ever."*

# Kipchoge Keino (KEN)

The "father of the Kenyan running tradition," two-time Olympic Champion 1968 and 1972; today, chairman of the National Olympic Committee of Kenya:

*"Paul Tergat is an athlete to be admired for what he has done for himself and for his country. I hope the youth will imitate his training, his mental preparation and his way of*

*life because he is the most disciplined and the most dedicated athlete we have ever produced in Kenya. He is a person to be admired considering his background and also from his way of handling things. This is a person we need to learn more from. We are very thankful for all his achievements and performances. We admire Paul Tergat for what he has done for us.*

*And he doesn't put his shoulders up. He is always humble and ready to talk and answer questions no matter where they come from. We wish him all the best for his future and we hope he will come back as a leader of athletics in this country so that others can be able to benefit more from his knowledge, his experience and his humanity."*

## Mike Kosgei (KEN)

Kenya's national coach in most of the years when Tergat won his five World Championship titles in cross country:

*"To me, Paul Tergat is the greatest athlete. What he has achieved on the track, on the road and in cross country is extraordinary. He has always been an athlete who was ready to listen and learn. He did not question the workouts. He was ready every minute. He is a role mode for the new generation, also because he is a very good person. He is a diplomat, a gentleman. He doesn't like controversies. He always liked clean things and problems to be put on the table.*

*This is him. Tergat always had everything that an athlete needs at the top."*

# Yobes Ondieki (KEN)

The first man who broke the 27-minute barrier at 10,000m (1993 in Oslo); World Champion at 5,000m, 1991:

*"As an athlete he has done a lot for the sport and for the country. He is the most celebrated cross country runner in the world. I thank God that he was the first Kenyan to break the marathon World Record and bring it under 2 hours five minutes. I think this in itself is a very big achievement. A few years ago, people never thought that somebody could run under 2:05. I wish he had gotten the Olympic medal in Athens to finish his great career with. As a person, he has a very genuine heart, a very big heart. He is doing a lot for the starving people, for the fight against landmines and many other things. He is a very humanitarian man. Because the world has bestowed Paul Tergat the honor of Ambassador on humanitarian grounds, he should serve without reservations."*

# Ibrahim Hussein (KEN)

In the 1980s, Kenya's only world class marathon runner apart from Douglas Wakiihuri, won marathons in Honolulu (1985 and 1986), New York (1987) and Boston (1988); today assistant general secretary of Athletics Kenya:

*"Some years ago, before he even ran his first marathon, I told him if there is anybody who is able to bring the World Record under 2:05 it is him. When I ran in the '80s there were no pacesetters, but I still managed to run 2:08,43. So I knew with pacemakers and an athlete of Tergat's caliber it would be possible to go under 2:05. He has accomplished*

*almost everything. I had a lot of faith in him, even in Athens. Unfortunately, it wasn't do be. But Paul took his fate like a real sportsman. At the same time, I know him as a very serious businessman and a very serious family man. He is very much committed. He doesn't make his statements just like that. I know for Paul Tergat there are so many things he would like to be changed in athletics. When he comes with a project it is always in a very sober-minded way. I am certain one of these days he will be a leader in the athletics association."*

## Brother Colm O'Connell (IRL)

He has lived in Kenya since the late '70s and coached a lot of athletes when they were at St-Patrick's High School at Iten, among them Peter Rono, Wilson Kipketer, Japhet Kimutai und the Chirchir brothers William and Cornelius:

*"Paul Tergat is somebody who has managed in life to get very close to that perfect balance by being a successful athlete, somebody who is able to combine his athletic talent with his family responsibilities and also as a role model. Paul is somebody who is easily recognized in Kenya, somebody who young people look up to. And I think he carries himself very well in public in that he is able to deal with people from the top right to the bottom. He can deal with the highest dignitaries and successful people, he can reach down to younger people in his village, young athletes who aspire to become Paul Tergat. For me, he is somebody who has really struck that perfect balance. All that has gone to make him what he is today, the success he is. Because he has managed to keep all the aspects of his life in place and in harmony."*

# Appendix

| | |
|---|---|
| Olympic Games: | 1996 Atlanta: 2nd 10,000m; 2000 Sydney: 2nd 10,000m; 2004 Athens: 10th marathon |
| World Championships: | 1995 Gothenburg: 3rd 10,000; 1997 Athens: 2nd 10,000m; 1999 Seville: 2nd 10,000m |
| Cross country WCh: | 1993 Amorebieta: 10th; 1994 Budapest: 4th; 1995 Durham; 1996 Stellenbosch; 1997 Turin; 1998 Marrakech and 1999 Belfast: 1st; 2000 Vilamoura: 3rd. Won a record number of 13 golds: 5 individual and 8 team medals |
| Half-marathon WCh: | 1992 Newcastle: 5th, 1994 Oslo: 11th, 1999 Palermo and 2000 Veracruz: 1st |
| World Records: | 10 000 m: 26:27,85, Brussels 1997; 15km road: 42:13, St. Denis 1994; 20km road: 56:18, Milan 1998; half-marathon: 59:17, Milan 1998 and 59:06, Lisbon 2000 (course 40m downhill); marathon: 2:04:55, Berlin 2003 |
| City Marathons: | 2001: 2nd London (2:08:14) and 2nd Chicago (2:08:50); 2002: 2nd London (2:05:48) and 4th Chicago (2:06:18); 2003 4th London (2:07:58) and 1st Berlin (2:04:55, WR) |

| Victory series: | 5 times World Cross country Champion 1995-1999; winner IAAF Cross Challenge 1996, 1997, 1998 and 2000; 22 cross country victories 1992-1999; 6 times winner Stramilano half-marathon in Milan 1994-1999; unbeaten over the half-marathon 1995-2000; 5 times winner Corrida de Sao Silvestre in Sao Paulo (15 km) 1995, 1996, 1998, 1999 and 2000 |
| --- | --- |

## Performance development:

| | 5000 m | 10.000 m | Marathon |
| --- | --- | --- | --- |
| 1991 (22) | | 29:46,8A | |
| 1992 (23) | 13:48,64 | | |
| 1993 (24) | 13:20,16 | 27:18,43 | |
| 1994 (25) | 13:15,07 | 27:23,89 | |
| 1995 (26) | 13:07,49 | 27:14,08 | |
| 1996 (27) | 12:54,72 | 26:54,41 | |
| 1997 (28) | 12:49,87 | 26,27,85 WR | |
| 1998 (29) | 12:58,74 | 26:44,44 | |
| 1999 (30) | 12:55,37 | 27:10,08 | |
| 2000 (31) | 12:55,18 | 27:03,87 | |
| 2001 (32) | | | 2:08:15 |
| 2002 (33) | | | 2:05:48 |
| 2003 (34) | | | 2:04:55 WR |
| 2004 (35) | | | 2:14:45* |

* competed only in the Olympic marathon

## Personal records:

| | |
|---|---|
| 1500m: | 3:42,3 (1996) |
| 1 Mile: | 3:58,4 (1996) |
| 2000m: | 4:57,4 (1996) |
| 3000m: | 7:28,70 (1996) |
| 5000m: | 12:49,87 (1997) |
| 10,000m: | 26:27,85 (1997, WR) |
| Half-marathon: | 59:17 (1998, WR) |
| | 59:06 (2000, unofficial WR) |
| | 58:51 (1996, Milan, course short by 49m) |
| Marathon: | 2:04:55 (2003, WR). |

## TERGAT'S PERSONAL DATA

| | |
|---|---|
| Date of birth: | June 17, 1969 |
| Place of birth: | Riwo (Baringo district, Kenya) |
| Tribe: | Tugen |
| Profession: | Athlete/Army (Officer 2 Air Force)/ Businessman |
| Residence: | Ngong (suburb of Nairobi) |
| Marital status: | married to Monica, 3 children: Ronald (1989), Harriet (1995) and Gloria (1999) |
| Coach: | Dr. Gabriele Rosa |
| Sponsor: | Nike |

# World Record HISTORY

**First man under 31 minutes:**
30:58,8   Jean Bouin (FRA)         16.11.11   Colombes

**First man under 30 minutes:**
29:52,6   Taisto Mäki (FIN)        17.09.39   Helsinki

**First man under 29 minutes:**
28:54,2   Emil Zatopek (TCH)       01.06.54   Brussels

**First man under 28 minutes:**
27:39,4   Ron Clarke (AUS)         14.07.65   Oslo

**Last 12 improvements:**

| | | | |
|---|---|---|---|
| 27:22,4 | Henry Rono (KEN) | 11.06.78 | Wien |
| 27:13,81 | Fernando Mamede (POR) | 02.07.84 | Stockholm |
| 27:08,23 | Arturo Barrios (MEX) | 18.08.89 | Berlin |
| 27:07,91 | Richard Chelimo (KEN) | 05.07.93 | Stockholm |
| 26:58,38 | Yobes Ondieki (KEN) | 10.07.93 | Oslo |
| 26:52,23 | William Sigei (KEN) | 22.07.94 | Oslo |
| 26:43,53 | Haile Gebrselassie (ETH) | 05.06.95 | Hengelo |
| 26:38,08 | Salah Hissou (MAR) | 23.08.96 | Brussels |
| 26:31,32 | Haile Gebrselassie (ETH) | 04.07.97 | Oslo |
| **26:27,85** | **Paul Tergat (KEN)** | **22.08.97** | **Brussels** |
| 26:22,75 | Haile Gebrselassie (ETH) | 01.06.98 | Hengelo |
| 26:20,31 | Kenenisa Bekele (ETH) | 08.06.04 | Ostrava |

*(First World Championship in 1992, before this there is not an official IAAF distance. Note: From the times listed below, the IAAF regognizes only the 2 from Milan.)*

| 60:55 | Mark Curp (USA) | 18.09.85 | Philadelphia |
|---|---|---|---|
| 60:43 | Mike Musyoki (KEN) | 08.06.86 | Newcastle |
| 60:34 | Steve Moneghetti (AUS) | 16.09.90 | Newcastle |
| 60:27 | Steve Moneghetti (AUS) | 26.01.92 | Tokyo |
| 60:24 | Benson Masya (KEN) | 20.09.92 | Newcastle WC |
| 60:06 | Steve Moneghetti (AUS) | 24.01.93 | Tokyo |
| 59:47 | Moses Tanui (KEN) | 03.04.93 | Milan |
| **59:17** | **Paul Tergat (KEN)** | **04.04.98** | **Milan** |
| **59:06** | **Paul Tergat (KEN)** | **26.03.00** | **Lisbon** |

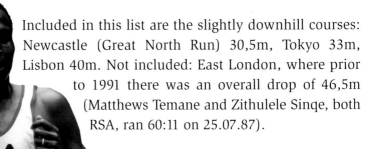

Included in this list are the slightly downhill courses: Newcastle (Great North Run) 30,5m, Tokyo 33m, Lisbon 40m. Not included: East London, where prior to 1991 there was an overall drop of 46,5m (Matthews Temane and Zithulele Sinqe, both RSA, ran 60:11 on 25.07.87).

**First man below 3:00h:**

2:55:18,4  John Hayes (USA)            24.07.08  London

**First man below 2:50h:**

2:46:52,8  James Clark (USA)           12.02.09  New York

**First man below 2:40h:**

2:38:16,2  Harry Green (GBR)           12.05.13  London

**First man below 2:30h:**

2:29:01,8  Albert Michelsen (USA)      12.10.25  Port Chester

**First man below 2:20h:**

2:18:40,4  James Peters (GBR)          13.06.53  Chiswick

**Last 12 improvements:**

2:12:11,2  Abebe Bikila (ETH)          13.06.64  Tokyo

2:12:00,0  Morio Shigematsu (JAP)      12.06.65  Chiswick

2:09.36,4  Derek Clayton (AUS)         06.12.67  Fukuoka

2:08:33,6  Derek Clayton (AUS)         30.05.69  Antwerpen

2:08:18    Rob de Castella (AUS)       06.12.81  Fukuoka

2:08:05    Steve Jones (GBR)           21.10.84  Chicago

2:07:12    Carlos Lopes (POR)          20.04.85  Rotterdam

2:06:50    Belayneh Dinsamo (ETH)      17.04.88  Rotterdam

2:06:05    Ronaldo Da Costa (BRA)      20.09.98  Berlin

2:05:42    Khalid Khannouchi (MAR)     24.10.99  Chicago

2:05:38    Khalid Khannouchi (USA)     14.04.02  London

2:04:55    Paul Tergat (KEN)           28.09.03  Berlin

# KENYAN World Record HOLDERS

## 3000m

| 7:39,6 | Kipchoge Keino | 27.08.65 Hälsingborg |
|--------|----------------|----------------------|
| 7:32,1 | Henry Rono | 27.06.78 Oslo |
| 7:28,96 | Moses Kiptanui | 16.08.92 Cologne |
| 7:20,67 | Daniel Komen | 01.09.96 Rieti |

**Record holder in spring 2005:**
| 7:20,67 | Daniel Komen (KEN) | 01.09.96 Rieti |
|---------|---------------------|----------------|

## 5000m

| 13:24,2 | Kipchoge Keino | 30.11.65 Auckland |
|---------|----------------|-------------------|
| 13:08,4 | Henry Rono | 08.04.78 Berkeley |
| 13:06,20 | Henry Rono | 13.09.81 Knarvik |
| 12:55,30 | Moses Kiptanui | 08.06.95 Rome |
| 12:39,74 | Daniel Komen | 22.08.97 Brussels |

**Record holder in spring 2005:**
| 12:37,35 | Kenenisa Bekele (ETH) | 31.05.04 Hengelo |
|----------|------------------------|-------------------|

## 10.000m

| 27:30,5 | Samson Kimobwa | 30.07.77 Helsinki |
|---------|----------------|-------------------|
| 27:22,4 | Henry Rono | 11.06.78 Vienna |
| 27:07,91 | Richard Chelimo | 05.07.93 Stockholm |
| 26:58,38 | Yobes Ondieki | 10.07.93 Oslo |
| 26:52,23 | William Sigei | 22.07.94 Oslo |
| **26:27,85** | **Paul Tergat** | **22.08.97 Brussels** |

**Record holder in spring 2005:**
| 26:20,31 | Kenenisa Bekele (ETH) | 08.06.04 Ostrava |
|----------|------------------------|-------------------|

## Half-marathon

| 60:24 | Benson Masya | 20.09.92 Newcastle |
|---|---|---|
| 59:47 | Moses Tanui | 03.04.93 Milan |
| 59:17 | Paul Tergat | 04.04.98 Milan |
| 59:06 | Paul Tergat | 26.03.00 Lisbon |

**Record holder in spring 2005:**

| 59:17 | Paul Tergat (KEN) | 04.04.98 Milan |
|---|---|---|

## Marathon

| 2:04:55 | Paul Tergat | 28.09.03 Berlin |
|---|---|---|

**Record holder in spring 2005:**

| 2:04:55 | Paul Tergat (KEN) | 28.09.03 Berlin |
|---|---|---|

## 3000m steeplechase

| 8:19,8 | Benjamin Jipcho | 19.06.73 Helsinki |
|---|---|---|
| 8:14,0 | Benjamin Jipcho | 27.06.73 Helsinki |
| 8:05,4 | Henry Rono | 13.05.78 Seattle |
| 8:05,35 | Peter Koech | 03.07.89 Stockholm |
| 8:02,08 | Moses Kiptanui | 19.08.92 Zurich |
| 7:59,18 | Moses Kiptanui | 16.08.95 Zurich |
| 7:59,08 | Wilson Boit Kipketer | 13.08.97 Zurich |
| 7:55,72 | Bernard Barmasai | 24.08.97 Cologne |

**Record holder in spring 2005:**

| 7:53,63 | Saif Saeed Shaheen (QAT, former Sephen Cherono, KEN) | 03.09.04 Brussels |
|---|---|---|

There has never been a Kenyan World Record holder at shorter distances than 3,000m. (Wilson Kipketer, 800m 1:41,11, is Kenyan born but running for Denmark.)

The only Kenyan women to break a World Record were Tegla Loroupe and Catherine Ndereba in marathon. In half-marathon, Susan Chepkemei ran 65:44 in Lisbon 2001, the fastest time in the world so far, but the course was 60m downhill. Therefore, the time was not recognized as a World Record.

## Marathon women:

| | | |
|---|---|---|
| 2:20:47 | Tegla Loroupe | 19.04.98 Rotterdam |
| 2:20:43 | Tegla Loroupe | 26.09.99 Berlin |
| 2:18:47 | Catherine Ndereba | 07.10.01 Chicago |

**Record holder in spring 2005:**

| | | |
|---|---|---|
| 2:15:25 | Paula Radcliffe (GBR) | 13.04.03 London |

# USEFUL ADDRESSES

## MARATHON ORGANIZERS

### JANUARY:

**Tiberias ISR**
Tiberias International
Marathon
iaa@internet-zahav.net
www.iaa.co.il

**Arizona USA**
Rock'n'Roll Arizona Marathon
info@rnraz.com
www.rnraz.com

**Orlando USA**
Walt Disney World Marathon
road.races@disney.com
www.disneyworldsports.com

**Houston USA**
Houston Marathon
marathon@hphoustonmaratho
n.com
www.hphoustonmarathon.com

### FEBRUARY:

**Cairo EGY**
Egyptian International
Marathon
info@egyptianmarathon.net
www.egyptianmarathon.net

**Seville ESP**
Seville Marathon
marathon@id.aytosevilla.org
www.marasevi.vianetworks.es

### MARCH:

**Barcelona ESP**
Marathon Catalunya
marathoncat@retemail.es
www.redestb.es

**Rome ITA**
Rome City Marathon
info@maratonadiroma.it
www.maratonadiroma.it

**Los Angeles USA**
Los Angeles Marathon
raceinfo@lamarathon.com
www.lamarathon.com

### APRIL:

**Paris FRA**
Paris International Marathon
info@parismarathon.com
www.parismarathon.com

**Madrid ESP**
Madrid Marathon
mapoma@arrakis.es
www.marathonmadrid.com

**Hamburg GER**
Marathon Hamburg
www.marathon-hamburg.com

**London GBR**
London Marathon
Fax +44/171 620 4208
www.london-marathon.co.uk

**Turin ITA**
Turin Marathon
info@turinmarathon.it
www.turinmarathon.it

**Rotterdam NED**
Rotterdam Marathon
info@rotterdammarathon.nl
www.rotterdammarathon.nl

**Zurich SUI**
Zurich Marathon
info@zurichmarathon.com
www.zurichmarathon.com

**Carmel USA**
Big Sur Marathon
info@bsim.org
www.bsim.org

**Boston USA**
Boston Marathon
mile27registration@baa.org
www.baa.org

**Nashville USA**
Country Music Marathon
cmm@eliteracing.com
www.cmmarathon.com

## MAY:

**Vienna AUT**
Vienna City Marathon
office@vienna-marathon.com
www.vienna-marathon.com

**Vancouver CAN**
Vancouver International
Marathon
info@vanmarathon.bc.ca
www.adidasvanmarathon.ca

## JUNE:

**Queensland AUS**
Gold Cost Marathon
www.goldcostmarathon.com.au

**Tromsö NOR**
Midnight Sun Marathon
post@msm.no
www.msm.no

**Stockholm SWE**
Stockholm Marathon
info@marathon.se
www.marathon.se

**San Diego USA**
Rock'n'Roll Marathon
rnrm@eliteracing.com
www.rnrmarathon.com

## JULY:

**Swiss Alpine Marathon**
info@alpine-davos.ch
www.swissalpine.ch

## AUGUST:

**Helsinki FIN**
Helsinki City Marathon
sul.harraste@sul.fi
www.helsinkicitymarathon.com

## SEPTEMBER:

**Sydney AUS**
Sydney Marathon
graeme.lannan@frontiersgroup
.com.au
www.sydneymarathon.org

**Pauillac FRA**
Marathon du Medoc
info@marathondumedoc.com
www.marathondumedoc.com

**Berlin GER**
Berlin Marathon
info@berlin-marathon.com
www.berlin-marathon.com

**Moscow RUS**
Moscow Marathon
fond@marafon.msk.ru
www.marafon.msk.ru

**Interlaken SUI**
Jungfrau Marathon
info@jungfrau-marathon.ch
www.jungfrau-marathon.ch

**Maui USA**
Maui Marathon
bark@maui.net
www.mauimarathon.com

## OCTOBER

**Toronto CAN**
Canadian International
Marathon
marathon@netcom.ca
www.torontomarathon.com

**Mallorca ESP**
Mallorca Marathon
info@marathon-pdm.com
www.Marathon-PDM.com

**Frankfurt GER**
Marathon Frankfurt
mail@frankfurt-marathon.com
www.frankfurt-marathon.com

**Munich GER**
Munich Marathon
info@mdienmarathon.de
www.medienmarathon.de

**Dublin IRL**
Dublin Marathon
bhaa@eircom.net
www.dublincitymarathon.ie

**Carpi ITA**
Italian Marathon
info@italianmarathon.it
www.italianmarathon.it

**Venice ITA**
Venice Marathon
info@venicemarathon.it
www.venicemarathon.it

**Amsterdam NED**
Amsterdam Marathon
info@ingamsterdammarathon.nl
www.ingamsterdammarathon.nl

**Lausanne SUI**
Olympic Marathon Lausanne
bruchez.robert@organisations.org
www.lausanne-marathon.com

**Chicago USA**
Chicago Marathon
Marathon@wwa.com
www.chicagomarathon.com

**Minneapolis USA**
Twin Cities Marathon
info@twincitiesmarathon.org
www.twincitiesmarathon.org

## NOVEMBER:

**Monaco MON**
Monaco Marathon
www.monacomarathon.org

**New York USA**
New York City Marathon
intl@nyrrc.org
www.nycmarathon.org

## DECEMBER

**Honolulu USA**
Honolulu Marathon
info@honolulumarathon.org
www.honoulumarathon.org

# FEDERATIONS

## NATIONAL:

**Australia:**
Athletics Australia,
Suite 22, Fawkner Tower,
431 St.Kilda Rd, Melbourne,
Victoria 3004
www.athletics.org.au

**Canada:**
Athletics Canada,
Suite 300-2197 Riverside Drive,
Ottawa, Ontario K1H 7X3
www.athleticscanada.com

**Ethiopia:**
Ethiopian Athletic Federation,
Addis Ababa Stadium,
P.O. Box 3241, Addis Ababa

**Ireland:**
The Athletic Association of
Ireland,
11 Prospect Road, Glasnevin,
Dublin 9
www.athleticsireland.ie

**Kenya:**
Athletics Kenya,
P.O. Box 46722.
00100 Nairobi
www.athleticskenya.org

**New Zealand:**
Athletics New Zealand,
P.O. Box 741, Wellington
www.athletics.org.nz

**South Africa:**
Athletics South Africa,
P.O. Box 2712, Houghton 2041
www.athletics.org.za

**United Kingdom:**
UK Athletics, Athletics House,
10 Harborne Road,
Edgbaston,
Birmingham B15 3AA
www.ukathletics.net

**USA:**
USA Track and Field,
P.O. Box 120,
Indianapolis,
Indiana 46206-0120
www.usatf.org

## INTERNATIONAL

**IAAF:**
International Association of
Athletics Federations,
17, rue Princesse Florestine,
BP 359, 98007 Monaco Cedex
www.iaaf.org

**AIMS:**
Association of International
Marathons and Road Races
www.aims-association.org

**World Mountain Running Association:**
www.wmra.info

**World Masters Athletics:**
www.world-masters-athletics.org

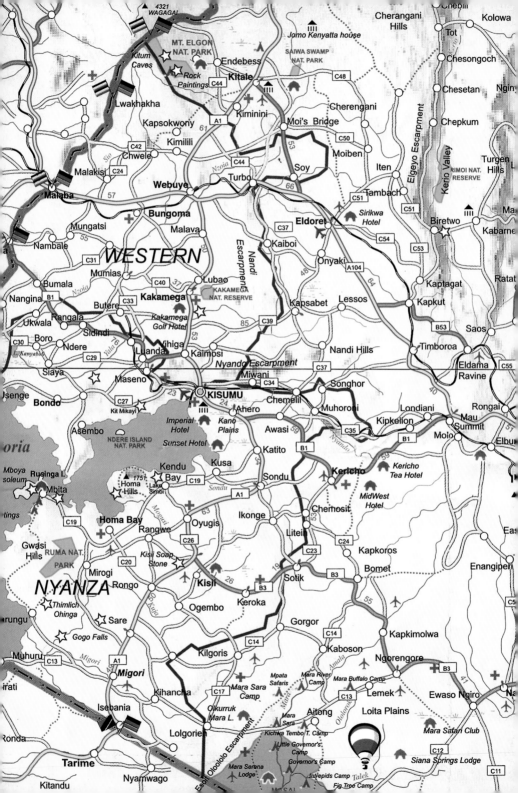

© Bundu Maps Services

# PHOTO CREDITS

Cover design: Jens Vogelsang

Cover photos: Sportpressephoto Bongarts, Germany; Jürg Wirz

Back cover photos: Jürg Wirz, Wendy Stone, Brian J. Myers, Gabriele Giugni, private archives of Paul Tergat

Inside photos:
Bongarts: pp. 12, 13 (top), 97
dpa/pa: p. 83, 114
Andreas Gonseth: pp. 25, 28, 43, 81, 112, 119, 121, 123, 145, 197
Jiro Mochizuki: p. 135
Omega/Colombo: pp. 52, 57, 58, 210
Ch. Rochard/L'Equipe: p. 84
Papon/L'Equipe: p. 128
Mutton: p. 96
Marc Herremans: pp. 86/87
Victor Sailer: p. 101
United Nations, World Food Program:
   Rein Skullerud: pp. 167, 177
   Wendy Stone: pp. 23, 166, 179
   Edward Parsons: pp. 9, 45, 201 (top)
   Gabriele Giugni: p. 200
   Francesco Broli: pp. 8, 175, 178, 199, 208
   Brian J. Myers: pp. 148-155

Official White House Photo: p. 183

All other photos are by Jürg Wirz and private photos from the archives of Paul Tergat

Map (pp. 220/221): Bundu Maps Services, Nairobi

Jeff Galloway
**Running**
Getting Started

232 pages, full color print
20 photos, 10 illustrations
Paperback, 5 $^3/4$" x 8 $^1/4$"
ISBN: 1-84126-166-1
c. £ 12.95 UK / $ 17.95 US
$ 26.95 CDN / € 16.95

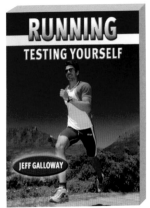

Jeff Galloway
**Running**
Testing Yourself

216 pages, full color print
20 photos, 10 illustrations
Paperback, 5 $^3/4$" x 8 $^1/4$"
ISBN: 1-84126-167-X
c. £ 12.95 UK / $ 17.95 US
$ 26.95 CDN / € 16.95

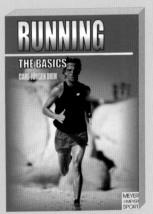

Carl-Jürgen Diem
**Running**
The Basics

168 pages, full-color print
5 photos, 82 illustrations, 5 tables
Paperback, 5 $^3/4$" x 8 $^1/4$"
ISBN 1-84126-139-4
£ 12.95 UK / $ 17.95 US
$ 25.95 CDN / € 16.90

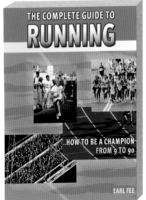

Earl Fee
**The
Complete
Guide to
Running**

440 pages, full color print
50 photos and illustrations
Paperback, 5 $^3/4$" x 8 $^1/4$"
ISBN: 1-84126-162-9
c. £ 17.95 UK / $ 29.00 US
$ 39.95 CDN / € 23.95

MEYER & MEYER Sport | sales@m-m-sports.com | www.m-m-sports.com

MEYER
&MEYER
SPORT

# New Studies in Athletics

Published quarterly by the IAAF, New Studies in Athletics is the magazine for anyone interested in coaches education, technical research, development information and bibliographic documentation.

Dedicated to the promotion of the latest practical, technical and scientific track and field research from around the world, each issue has a special topic and a practical theme and includes:

- Articles on the world wide development of athletics;
- Reports from international congresses, seminars and symposia;
- Color photographs of the world's best athletes.

✂

## Subscription Form

Please accept my subscription order for NEW STUDIES IN ATHLETICS (calender year only)

Name _____

Address _____

Zip, City, Country _____

☐ Visa   ☐ Mastercard

Number: ☐☐☐☐ ☐☐☐☐ ☐☐☐☐ ☐☐☐☐   Expiry Date: ☐☐ ☐☐

CVC Number: (The **last 3 digits** of the number on the back of your card: ☐☐☐)

Date, Signature _____

Annual subscription rate in US$ 45.- (plus US$ 20.- airmail/US$ 9.- surface mail).
Make payments by credit card, international money order or postal order and send to:
Meyer & Meyer Sport • Von-Coels-Str. 390 • D-52080 Aachen • Germany
Phone: +49/241/9 58 10-0 • Fax: +49/241/9 58 10 10
E-mail: verlag@m-m-sports.com • http://www.m-m-sports.com
A few numbers of back issues (up to volume 12, 1997) are available on request from IAAF for US$ 10 each. Please remit your orders to the IAAF office in Monaco.

MEYER & MEYER Sport | sales@m-m-sports.com | www.m-m-sports.com